Often our university is seen as the campus—the buildings—the physical location where students, faculty and administrators gather to accomplish the work of higher education. In fact, it is the people who make the university a special place: its many knowledgable and committed faculty who have come and stayed, the students who attended, and the community who have supported the idea of a university for Hampton Roads for more than fifty years. Those people have molded Old Dominion University into a comprehensive state-assisted university with a mission for Hampton Roads, Virginia, the nation, and the world.

To the people who made the difference at Old Dominion we dedicate this first pictorial history. The history is not only a representation of our past, but is also a road map for the future. Alumni are not the guardians of the past but the guardians of the future. In that role, the Old Dominion University Alumni Association is pleased to present to you *Old Dominion University: Heritage and Horizons*, a celebration of the success of our university's past and of her future.

Designed by Sharon Varner Moyer

OLD DOMINION UNIVERSITY
Heritage and Horizons

By Richard A. Rutyna & John W. Kuehl

The Donning Company Publishers

February, 1963
The following is the description of the university seal as it was adopted by the Board of Visitors.

The central portion is a modified and simplified version of the Stuart arms, royal arms of the Stuart rulers at the time Virginia became known as the Old Dominion; the shields of the four kingdoms, England, Scotland, Ireland and France (which England still claimed). Over this has been placed the shield of the arms of the College of William and Mary, granted by the Heralds' College in 1694, to indicate our origin. Within concentric circles around the shields is the name of the University and date of its founding, "Old Dominion University – 1930."

The entire arrangement is to constitute the official seal of the University and is to be used on all official records and other documents requiring the use of a seal.

Copyright © 1987 by Richard A. Rutyna and John W. Kuehl

All rights reserved, including the right to reproduce this work in any form whatsoever without permission in writing from the publisher, except for brief passages in connection with a review. For information, write:

>The Donning Company/Publishers
>5659 Virginia Beach Boulevard
>Norfolk, Virginia 23502

Edited by Tony Lillis

Library of Congress Cataloging-in-Publication Data

Rutyna, Richard A.
  Old Dominion University.

  Includes index.
  1. Old Dominion University—History. 2. Old Dominion University—Description—Views.
I. Kuehl, John W. II. Title.
LD4331.R88   1987.   378.755'523   87-6667
ISBN 0-89865-531-5 (lim. ed.)

Printed in the United States of America

Contents

Foreword 7
Acknowledgments 8
Introduction 11

Chapter 1
Foundations 13

Chapter 2
Friends and Benefactors 35

Chapter 3
The Classroom and Community 45

Chapter 4
Distinguished Alumni 69

Chapter 5
Student Life 77

Chapter 6
Athletics 143

Sports Halls of Fame 175
Appendix A 192
Appendix B 194
Appendix C 195
Appendix D 196
Index 197
About the Authors 200

Foreword

G. William Whitehurst

For anyone who is privileged to have been a part of the early Old Dominion family, this book will provide a nostalgic journey through the past. Former students and faculty members alike will relive their careers and experiences and be reminded of the special place this institution has in their hearts. Neighbors and friends in the community who have never had any formal affiliation with Old Dominion will also enjoy reading this work, because the history of Old Dominion is a story of community commitment as well. It is a story of fulfilled dreams and the promise of a bright future.

I began my association with the university in 1950 as a young instructor in the history department, when the school was still the Norfolk Division of William and Mary – Virginia Polytechnic Institute, or simply "The Division," as it was affectionately called. I am not sure anyone then other than Lewis Webb foresaw our growing into a four-year college, much less a full-fledged university. It took his vision and the support of some great friends of the school in the community to make that dream a reality.

I remember the excitement in the mid-1950s when it became apparent that our school was going to acquire its own identity and enter the ranks of the four-year institutions in our state. I recall the pride in our new name and the realization in the early 1960s that there really was a boundless future ahead. Under President Webb's able successors, James Bugg, Alfred Rollins, and now Joseph Marchello, Old Dominion University has achieved the academic preeminence that is the mark of a strong university. This became most apparent to me when I returned to the campus after an eighteen-year absence: the heart of the school beats to a new rhythm.

There is a richness in the university offerings that reflects imagination and unfettered initiative. There is no other word for it: to be a part of Old Dominion University now is an adventure. The reader will sense that when he has finished this book. Richard Rutyna and John Kuehl deserve high marks not only for their scholarship but for their ability to tell the Old Dominion story in a heartwarming and sensitive fashion.

Our first and greatest debt is to our colleague in the Old Dominion University history department, James R. Sweeney, whose golden anniversary history *Old Dominion University: A Half Century of Service* has been a very valuable source of information. To those who enjoy reading good narrative history and wish to know more about some of the things touched upon in this pictorial, we highly recommend his book.

President Joseph M. Marchello has encouraged our efforts with his enthusiastic support of this project. We are also grateful to Cynthia B. Duncan, dean of library services, for allowing us liberal access to the photograph collection in the University Archives. Susan Ellen Emser, operations manager of the University Archives, has been extremely helpful to us. Her knowledge of the collection she manages has saved us many hours of work and has allowed us to track down many elusive bits of information of the sort that make this kind of a history informative and worthwhile. Most of the photographs which appear herein have come from the collection in the University Archives. Others have come from the collections held by the Office of Public Information Services or the Office of Sports Information. A few have been provided by friends in the community. We have recognized each of these sources in the caption credit line which accompanies each photograph, and have cited the photographer as often as he or she was known to us. We are particularly grateful to the photographers who have worked in the Office of Public Information Services over the years. The

Acknowledgments

storehouse of photographic materials which they have presented to the university while in its employ has made this work possible.

Several people in the Office of Public Information Services have been helpful, but none more than Steve Daniel, editor of the *Alumnews*, and Robert Firek. Steve has been an excellent source of information and has aided us on numerous occasions when we were looking for a specific photograph, and Bob has shot a number of pictures for us and located and duplicated others for us as well. We owe both Steve and Bob a great deal.

David T. Shufflebarger, university vice president for advancement, has been very generous in sharing his limited time with us. His intimate knowledge of the history of the university, and of some of the most important people in its history, has been an invaluable guide to us. Benjamin F. Clymer, Jr., in the Office of Advancement, has also been most helpful to us, especially in acquiring several pictures without which we thought this pictorial would be less useful as a historical anthology.

Many people have been helpful in responding to our inquiries about specific details. These include a number of university alumni and other friends of the university, among whom A. Rufus Tonelson stands out. His assistance in identifying some individuals for whom no identification was otherwise available is much appreciated by us. Many university staff personnel have assisted us in too many ways to relate here, from Debbie LaMori who has done typing for us, to Dorothy June McLane, who has supplied us with important statistical information concerning the university. To those named, and to the many others not named, we extend our grateful thanks.

We also wish to express our appreciation to James Jarrett, director of athletics, Debbie Harmison Byrne, assistant director of athletics for public relations, and Carol R. Hudson, director of sports information, for the photographs and information which they have supplied to us. Their permission to use their photographs and the assistance they have rendered us with regard to sports information have been very helpful in writing the final chapter. The special section on the Old Dominion University Sports Hall of Fame is almost entirely the product of their labors. We thank them for their permission to use their pictures and their captions.

Finally, but certainly not least of all, we wish to express our appreciation to Gordon A. McDougall, the director of alumni relations, Margaret B. Holland, assistant director of alumni relations, Bernie Kirsch, president of the Alumni Association, and to the board of directors of the Alumni Association and the members of the association's history project committee. They have each and every one been helpful, supportive, considerate with their advice, and patient with our problems. This is in a very real sense their project, though the authors alone accept full responsibility for any shortcomings it may reflect.

Richard A. Rutyna
John W. Kuehl

Introduction

I am delighted to contribute to Old Dominion University's first pictorial history, *Old Dominion University: Heritage and Horizons*. Though a young institution, Old Dominion's contributions to Hampton Roads, the commonwealth of Virginia, and the nation, have been many. When one thinks of great universities, one thinks of outstanding faculty, of bright and promising students, of great repositories of learning, of attractive and functional physical facilities, and perhaps most importantly of all, of an intellectual spirit that pervades the everyday life of the institution. So it is here.

Old Dominion University exists today because fifty-six years ago eastern Virginians needed it, demanded it, and worked hard to achieve it. They envisioned an institution of higher learning that would foster democracy, individuality, and prosperity in the midst of the Great Depression and the Second World War. It could not create prosperity, but it did enrich the region culturally and educationally, and it laid the groundwork for the tremendous growth that would sweep the region forward in the years ahead. In a very real sense, then, the university belongs to the region and to the people whose dreams it actualized.

The institution which emerged from the post-war period had a unique mission to serve the people of southeastern Virginia. That mission has gradually been broadened without diminishing the original purpose for which the university was established. The programs at Old Dominion University have grown in both quantity and quality. Our university now offers bachelor's degrees in seventy-six areas, master's degrees in forty-six areas, and doctorates in twelve. There are many outstanding activities in arts and letters, business and public administration, education, engineering and technology, sciences and technology, and the health professions. These quality programs have sent thousands of trained citizens into the community where they have enriched the lives of their fellows. Through the training which they have received in the liberal arts, teachers, businessmen, nurses, doctors, engineers, and scientists have demonstrated their ability to think critically, to appreciate the arts and humanities, to cherish their cultural and political heritage, and to participate in their society.

The Board of Visitors, administration, faculty, and staff all deserve great credit for the fine institution that has been created and nourished here. As Benjamin Disraeli defined it, a university is a place of light, liberty, learning, and intellectual encounter. It is a place where people prepare for the future, fulfill their present, and grow through experimentation and creativity. Consequently, the university's worth can be measured in the final analysis only by its impact on the individual. To the extent that it is a place where students learn and the faculty engage in research and teaching, it benefits the state and nation as it disseminates knowledge in the community where its services have extended.

As you read Old Dominion's first pictorial history and savor the warm memories of the institution's success, I hope that you will also think about the potential for its future. The great work that has been accomplished and which is described in this book is an ideal platform upon which all of us may build an even greater university of international renown. Enjoy and treasure this history and continue to support Old Dominion University as it faces the challenges of the twenty-first century.

Joseph M. Marchello
President, Old Dominion University

Acquired as a gift from the city of Norfolk, March 13, 1930, the old Larchmont School building, which had been built in 1912, became the Norfolk Division of the College of William and Mary's all-purpose campus center. The trolley tracks which ran just in front of the building bore witness to the principal mission of the institution, which was to serve the residents of the region as a commuter college providing low cost quality education. Classes commenced at the college in September 1930. Virginia Polytechnic Institute began offering courses at the college, in a further joint venture, the following September. The old elementary school building ended its long and useful career as the Academic Building and was razed in 1975. The site where it stood is now a greenspace. Courtesy of University Archives

Chapter 1

Foundations

The history of Old Dominion University began in 1930 when the school was established as a branch of the College of William and Mary. It began in one old, abandoned public school building which college planners were able to secure with the help of good friends in the community. Created in response to a community need, and designed by community leaders to provide higher education to Norfolk and the surrounding area, the university has developed in partnership with the community which it serves. The "Norfolk Division" as it was then called began classes in September 1930 with 206 students.

By 1986, the college had grown into a major regional urban university, serving primarily the population of southeastern Virginia. The main Norfolk campus occupied 160 acres on the Elizabeth River, with additional educational centers either being established already or planned for the Hampton and Newport News peninsula, Virginia Beach, and the tri-city area of Portsmouth, Chesapeake, and Suffolk. In the fall semester of 1985-1986, more than fifteen thousand students were enrolled in the university.

As the university prepared to celebrate its twenty-fifth anniversary as an independent institution, February 16, 1987, it was making rapid strides toward becoming a national and even international institution of distinction. In 1985, *U.S. News and World Report* published a report in which college presidents ranked Old Dominion University among the ten best comprehensive institutions in its class in the South. A major reorganization was undertaken in 1986 to elevate the university's stature, and the existing schools were re-organized into several colleges. They are the College of Arts and Letters; the College of Business and Public Administration; the Darden College of Education; the College of Engineering and Technology; the College of Health Sciences; and the College of Sciences. Focusing upon what are termed "peaks of excellence" or areas of special emphasis, the university offered doctorates in twelve areas. Master's degrees were available in forty-six fields, and undergraduate students had a choice among seventy-six majors. A partner in the Virginia Center for Innovative Technology, the university was also engaged in research in such futuristic fields as robotics, ergonomics (man and machine studies in applied psychology) and artificial intelligence, the last of which engaged as many as twenty-three faculty members in five different departments. New emphases in such fields as world trade were being added to such established programs as public administration and oceanography. The university also continued its close working relationship with the National Aeronautics and Space Administration (NASA) at Langley. The university likewise continued to make a substantial contribution to the artistic and cultural life of the community, with plans being made for the construction of a new Fine Arts Center.

Proud of its heritage and the accomplishments of its past, Old Dominion University looks forward with eager anticipation to its future and to the horizons of intellectual and cultural achievement which lie before it.

In the beginning Old Dominion University was little more than a vacant lot and a dream. In this aerial view, looking north along Hampton Boulevard, the old Larchmont School can be seen at the bend in the road. Across the street was the new Larchmont School, the construction of which made the city of Norfolk's donation of the older building to the budding college a possibility. Early students at the college sometimes ate their lunch in the new elementary school cafeteria. Courtesy of University Archives

The campus building with the most unusual history is undoubtedly the Rehearsal Hall, which is located east of Hampton Boulevard on 47th Street. Commonly referred to as "The Stable" the building was acquired from the Virginia National Guard in 1965 and subsequently modernized in 1976. It is used as a rehearsal hall by music students. Built around 1916, The Stable was used as precisely that by the Norfolk Light Infantry Blues during World Wars I and II. Courtesy of Public Information Services; photograph by Robert Firek

The Norfolk Light Infantry Blues polo team, shown in this 1925 photograph, stabled some of their horses in what is now the Rehearsal Hall. From the Carroll H. Walker Collection

Some old landmarks associated with the university have changed in appearance over the years. In this 1920s vintage photograph, looking south down Hampton Boulevard, at the corner of 48th Street, Gray's Pharmacy can be seen in the center of the picture. From the Carroll H. Walker Collection

In another view of Gray's Pharmacy, which is at the right in this 1920s photograph, a trolley car rounds the corner at 48th Street preparing to turn on to Hampton Boulevard, which was then known as Myers Avenue. From the Carroll H. Walker Collection

A section of Hampton Boulevard near 47th Street can be seen in this picture which dates from about 1926. From the Carroll H. Walker Collection

Born in the first year of the Great Depression, the "Norfolk Division," as the college came to be known, was a beneficiary of federal funding under the New Deal programs of President Franklin D. Roosevelt. Public Works Administration (PWA) funds provided needed support for the construction of the Administration Building which was occupied in September, 1936. The name of the building was actually somewhat misleading as it contained not only administrative offices but also classrooms, the college library, two gymnasiums, and a swimming pool. Subsequent additions on the back side of the building provided added space. Funds made available by the Works Progress Administration (WPA) were used to beautify the campus. Seen here just beyond the south end of the Administration Building was Foreman Field. Courtesy of University Archives

The WPA and the Virginia Relief Administration provided funds to build the football stadium on land given to the college by the city. The stadium, shown under construction in this aerial view, was named for A. H. Foreman, who was an early advocate on behalf of the college. The stadium, which seated about 17,500 fans, was dedicated October 3, 1936. From the Carroll H. Walker Collection

Funds from the WPA also made possible the construction of the serpentine wall which bordered the expanding college campus along the west side of Hampton Boulevard in front of the Administration Building and what is now known as The Williamsburg Lawn. In the background in this 1930s photograph is the new Larchmont School. Courtesy of University Archives

The Science Building, completed in 1954, enabled science classes to move out of the cramped old Larchmont School building. A wing was soon added behind the south end of the building to accommodate a bookstore, snack bar, and cafeteria. The snack bar promptly came to be known as the "New Bud's" replacing the old "Bud's" which was in the Administration Building. Courtesy of University Archives

This aerial photograph of the Norfolk Division campus was taken between 1948 and 1954. Looking north toward the Science Building (1) as the old Larchmont School was then called, the photograph also shows the Administration Building (2) and Foreman Field (5). Two military-style, barracks-type buildings were acquired from the Federal Works Agency and erected on the southern edge of the campus in 1948. One of these became the Academic Building (3), later the home of the Division of Business Administration, and finally the Social Studies Building. It was razed in 1971 to make room for the new Administration Building. The other served as the home of the Technical Institute (4), which had been established in 1945. In 1959 the Technical Institute moved to a new building east of Hampton Boulevard between 46th Street and 47th Street, and the wooden frame structure was demolished in 1961. Some classes were conducted in the spaces under the east and west stands of the stadium. Also in the area east and southeast of the stadium were a number of frame and tar paper "shacks" which were utilized as classrooms, offices, and laboratories. The last of the shacks survived until the mid 1950s. Courtesy of University Archives; photograph by Photo Craftsmen, Inc.

The Hughes Library which was erected in 1958 was the first modern-style building to adorn the campus as it expanded southward. Noted for its distinctive solar screen exterior, the library was named for Robert Morton Hughes who was instrumental in the establishment of the Norfolk Division in 1930. Courtesy of Public Information Services

The first floor of the Hughes Library featured open stacks and well-lighted congenial work areas, typical of which was the reference area, shown here. The second floor was used for classrooms. The building continued to serve the university community as a library until 1976, at which time the new university library was opened. Hughes Hall, as the building is presently called, houses the Computer Center and the Center for Instructional Development, as well as other activities. Courtesy of University Archives

The Fine Arts Building was erected on the north side of the mall, next to the Hughes Library, in 1959. Designed to house the art and music departments, the building also became the repository for the Elise N. Hofheimer Art Library in 1982. Courtesy of University Archives

J. A. C. Chandler Memorial Hall, which was designed to house the departments of business administration, math, and physics, was opened in February, 1963. The building was named for the president of the College of William and Mary, 1919 to 1934, who played a vital role in the establishment of the Norfolk Division of the College of William and Mary in 1930. Courtesy of University Archives

Admiral Alvin D. Chandler, on the left, son of J. A. C. Chandler, for whom the School of Business Administration building was named, reflected with Lt. Gov. Mills E. Godwin, Jr., and President Lewis W. Webb, Jr., on the contribution of his father to the founding of the Norfolk Division, at the dedication of the building in May, 1963. Godwin, in the center, is a Distinguished Alumnus of the university and served two terms as governor of the commonwealth of Virginia. Courtesy of University Archives

The Charles L. Kaufman Engineering Hall opened in 1964. The building was named for one of the university's leading benefactors. Mr. Kaufman was a member of the Advisory Board throughout the fifteen years of its existence. Courtesy of University Archives; photograph by Carl Lindemann

From left to right were the dean of the School of Engineering, J. Harold Lampe; the first rector of the Board of Visitors, Frank Batten; Virginia legislator, Col. James W. Roberts; and university benefactor Charles L. Kaufman, at the dedication of the Kaufman Engineering Hall, April 29, 1965. Courtesy of University Archives

The February, 1965 demolition of John's College Restaurant, which was situated just east of the Hughes Library on Hampton Boulevard, marked the end of an era. Many former students no doubt have fond memories of meals and other "refreshments" served at John's, which was reportedly one of only three on-campus taverns in the nation at the time. Courtesy of University Archives

The centerpiece of the university campus is Webb Center, named for Lewis W. Webb, Jr. Webb came to the Norfolk Division in 1932, became its director in 1946, and became president of the independent Old Dominion College in 1962. He then presided over the transformation of the college into a university before retiring in 1969. Old Dominion University is in many ways the school built by the engineer Lewis W. Webb, Jr. Following his retirement as president, Webb returned to the classroom to teach physics.

Webb Center, which stands at the west end of Kaufman Mall, began operations in May, 1966. The building has since been expanded and includes the bookstore, cafeterias, the Rathskeller, game rooms, meeting rooms, and the offices of a variety of student organizations such as the Mace and Crown, *the student newspaper, and the Student Senate. Courtesy of Public Information Services*

This 1967 aerial photograph gives an excellent overview of the campus, looking northeast. The large H-shaped buildings east of Hampton Boulevard are student dormitories, Rogers Hall and Gresham Hall. The large building in the foreground is Webb Center. The buildings along the south side of the mall had not been completed when this photograph was taken. The building under construction in the lower right corner of the picture was the John S. Alfriend Chemistry Building. Courtesy of University Archives; photograph by Perry Breon

The John S. Alfriend Chemistry Building opened in 1967. Mr. Alfriend, a leading area banker, served as a member of the Advisory Board for the Norfolk Division from 1947 to 1962. He was a member of the Educational Foundation from 1962 to 1974 and served as president of that body from 1962 to 1971. Courtesy of University Archives

Mayor Roy B. Martin, Jr., ('40) of Norfolk, on the left, was greeted by John S. Alfriend at the dedication of the Alfriend Chemistry Building in July, 1967. Courtesy of University Archives

The Child Study Center, shown in the foreground, was dedicated March 23, 1967. The center was made possible with funds donated by the Kiwanis and Lions clubs of the area. Speech and hearing clinics were located in the center as well as a facility for training teachers of visually handicapped children. Courtesy of Public Information Services

In 1968, a major addition to the Technical Institute complex was completed. The original building, which was located between 46th Street and 47th Street on the east side of Hampton Boulevard, was erected in 1959. The addition, shown here, provided classroom space as well as a large theater-auditorium. Also located in the building was the university's nationally-acclaimed dental hygiene program, sponsored by the Virginia Tidewater Dental Association Foundation and dedicated September 1, 1968.

Between 1965 and 1969, technical-vocational education was de-emphasized by the university. An expanding community college system throughout the state, and the establishment of a technical-vocational school in Norfolk, precluded the necessity for the university to continue offering classes in more than a few specialized areas. Some programs such as dental hygiene became full four-year programs while others were taken over by an academic school. Courtesy of University Archives; photograph by Jim Dillinger

This modest building on 49th Street, known affectionately as "Fink's Flats," was the first home of the School of Education. The name was a tribute to T. Ross Fink, who became the first dean of the Darden School of Education in 1963. After the School of Education moved to more commodious quarters on the south side of the mall, this building served as home for the Department of Political Science, and subsequently as headquarters for Campus Security until it was demolished to make way for the new Public Safety Building. Courtesy of University Archives

The Darden School of Education moved into new quarters on the mall in 1969. The school was named for former congressman and governor, Colgate W. Darden, Jr., who with his wife, Constance, has been a loyal friend and benefactor of the university. Courtesy of University Archives; photograph by Tom Miracle

The field house, also known as the Health and Physical Education Building, opened in fall 1970. The men's basketball team played its home games in this facility before moving to Scope in downtown Norfolk. The women's basketball team continued to utilize the facility for its home games. In addition, the building houses the offices of the athletic director and his staff, and serves as the nerve center for the university's diversified sports programs. Courtesy of Public Information Services

Duckworth Memorial Hall was completed October 6, 1971. The building, which was used by the School of Engineering, was named for William Frederick Duckworth, who was a mayor of Norfolk and a good friend of the university during its formative years. Courtesy of Public Information Services

The Arts and Letters Building was completed June 1, 1972. In 1976, it was named for Frank Batten who served the university as a member of the Advisory Board and the Board of Visitors from 1955 to 1973. Batten was the first rector of the Board of Visitors, from 1962 to 1970. Courtesy of Public Information Services

The new Administration Building, which was built on the site of the former Social Studies Building, opened in 1972. The old Administration Building subsequently came to serve as the registration center and office of student records. Courtesy of University Archives

This 1972 aerial view of the campus, looking west toward the Elizabeth River, shows the recently completed nine-story Arts and Letters Building on the left. The buildings along the south side of the mall had been completed by this date, as had the field house, which is shown at the top of the picture. Rogers Hall residence dormitory is shown at the lower right. The new Administration Building which also opened in 1972 is shown just east of Foreman Field. Courtesy of University Archives

The plaza in front of Webb Center features the Fountain of Organized Labor, which was donated to the university April 24, 1976, by the Greater Tidewater Virginia Central Labor Council AFL-CIO. Courtesy of Public Information Services

Representatives of organized labor who participated in the dedication of the fountain on the plaza in front of Webb Center were, left to right, Carl B. Hough, Paul A. Askew, John H. Drummond, Sr., Julian F. Carper, and Gene E. Leach. Courtesy of University Archives; photograph by Steve Shires

Campus development can be unsightly and inconvenient at times, as this photograph of the mall under construction depicts. Work on the mall was completed in the late 1970s, after what often seemed interminable delays. The mall was dedicated by university President James L. Bugg, Jr., in April 1976, and was named Kaufman Mall, for Mr. and Mrs. Charles L. Kaufman, at the request of their son and daughter-in-law, George and Linda Kaufman, whose generous support made the eventual beautification of Kaufman Mall possible. Courtesy of University Archives; photograph by V. L. Gary

The University Library, which stands between the Batten Arts and Letters Building and the Godwin Life Sciences Building, opened May 17, 1976. The four-story modern building housed more than 600,000 volumes and offered advanced library services. Courtesy of Public Information Services

31

The Godwin Life Sciences Building opened for classes in January, 1981. The building is named for a Distinguished Alumnus and former governor of the commonwealth of Virginia, Mills E. Godwin, Jr. Courtesy of Public Information Services

The new Public Safety Building opened on campus in February, 1984. Standing on the site previously occupied by "Fink's Flats," it is located on 49th Street just south of the new Administration Building. Courtesy of Public Information Services

In 1986, a connecting structure was built between Duckworth Memorial Hall and the Charles L. Kaufman Engineering Hall. The new construction brought the School of Engineering under one roof and provided additional space for classrooms, laboratories, and offices. Courtesy of Public Information Services

The university opened its Peninsula Graduate Center in August, 1986. Established to better serve the residents of Newport News, Hampton, and the other cities and counties of the peninsula, the center began its operations by offering graduate courses in engineering. Courtesy of Public Information Services

Mrs. Fay Martin Slover, the widow of Samuel LeRoy Slover, who was mayor of Norfolk in the 1930s, has been the most generous benefactor of the university in its slightly more than fifty year history. The daughter of the Alvah Martins, an eminent Norfolk family, Mrs. Slover was associated with her husband in the development of the communications corporation which published the Norfolk Virginian Pilot and Norfolk Ledger-Dispatch newspapers and which also operated the WTAR radio and television stations. Following the death of her husband in 1959, Mrs. Slover's nephew, Frank Batten, assumed the positions of publisher and board chairman of the corporate enterprise. When Mrs. Slover died in 1967, she bequeathed what has grown to an $8,400,000 endowment to the university to be used primarily for the development of the program in oceanography. Courtesy of Frank Batten

Chapter 2

Friends and Benefactors

Since the 1920s, many friends have given of themselves to the university and are a part of the heritage of the institution. Some of them have been featured in the previous chapter. In this chapter, others who have helped shape the school's development from the Norfolk Division of the College of William and Mary and Virginia Polytechnic Institute, into Old Dominion University are pictured. As benefactors, they have given focus to the horizons of a great university.

On those occasions when special recognition has been warranted for exceptional service to Old Dominion, the University Medal has been awarded. It is given in tribute of special service that has brought distinction to Old Dominion University and furthered its pursuit of excellence. The University Medal is Old Dominion's highest award, and is given only by the authority of the president and the Board of Visitors.

The medallion is a slightly reduced replica of the one worn by the president of the university during ceremonial occasions and signifies the office of president of Old Dominion University. The original medal was authorized by the Board of Visitors in 1976 and first worn by Alfred B. Rollins, Jr., at his inauguration as the university's third president. The first replica was presented in 1978 to honor Colgate W. Darden, Jr., former governor of Virginia. Others who have earned the award are Charles L. Kaufman (1978); Frank Batten (1980); Lewis W. Webb, Jr., (1980); Elise N. and Henry Clay Hofheimer II (1982); George M. and Linda H. Kaufman (1986); Virginia Rice Webb (1986); Harry Hirsch Mansbach (1986); and Robert L. Fodrey, Sr., (1986).

One of the founding fathers of the university, Robert M. Hughes worked hard during the 1920s to make the Norfolk Division of the College of William and Mary a reality. Between 1893 and 1917, he was a member of the Board of Visitors of William and Mary. In 1925, Hughes suggested the need for a two year branch of the college in Norfolk. He continued to work through the College Committee of the Norfolk-Portsmouth Chamber of Commerce to achieve that goal. The Hughes Library was named in his honor. Courtesy of University Archives

From left to right, President J. A. C. Chandler, Governor John Garland Pollard, Mrs. W. M. Cooke, Norfolk Mayor S. Heth Tyler, and Mrs. Franz Naylor are pictured on October 29, 1930, as they prepared to celebrate Chandler's and Mrs. Naylor's birthdays. The celebration also marked the inauguration of the William and Mary-Norfolk Ledger-Dispatch course in public affairs at the Woman's Club, of which Mrs. Naylor was president. Mayor Tyler was instrumental in the city of Norfolk's donation of the old Larchmont School to the new Norfolk Division in 1930. Courtesy of University Archives

J. A. C. Chandler was the president of the College of William and Mary who supported the establishment of the two year branch of the college in Norfolk. On June 13, 1930, he announced that the Norfolk Division would become a reality. Chandler was an enthusiastic supporter of the Norfolk campus. Chandler Hall was named in his honor. Courtesy of University Archives

Joseph E. Healy, director of the William and Mary extension program in Norfolk and principal of Blair Junior High School, was a leader in the movement to establish a branch of the College of William and Mary in Norfolk, and assisted in securing the old Larchmont School building for the new campus extension. Courtesy of University Archives

A. H. Foreman, chairman of the Norfolk School Board and a member of the Board of Visitors of the College of William and Mary, played a key role in helping to secure the old Larchmont School building for the use of the new Norfolk Division. He was also tireless in efforts to obtain funding for the campus stadium which bears his name. Courtesy of University Archives

Norfolk Mayor William Frederick Duckworth, second from the right, was made an honorary member of the Political Club at the Norfolk Division when he spoke at the January 17, 1958 meeting. "Fred" Duckworth, for whom Duckworth Memorial Hall was named, was a very good friend of the young college and played a major role in securing land south of 49th Street for expansion of the campus. Shown with the mayor are, left to right, E. Vernon Peele, dean of instruction, Marie Chatham and Robert L. Stern, sponsors of the club, and Milton Parsons, president of the club. Courtesy of University Archives

Running for Virginia's top state offices when they visited the campus in 1961 were then State Senator Mills E. Godwin, Jr., left, candidate for lieutenant governor, Attorney General Albertis S. Harrison, Jr., center, candidate for governor, and State Senator Robert Y. Button, right, candidate for attorney general. Harrison was governor of the commonwealth when the university attained independence in 1962 and played a vital role in garnering the necessary votes for independence in the state legislature at a time when there was considerable opposition to the plan. Shown with the successful candidates were G. William Whitehurst of the history department, second from the left, and President Lewis W. Webb, Jr., second from the right. Courtesy of University Archives

Guests at the dedication of the Webb Center on May 20, 1966, were, left to right, Mrs. and Mr. Harvey L. Lindsay and Mrs. and Mr. Charles Marshall, Jr. Mrs. Lindsay served on the first Board of Visitors of the independent college. Courtesy of University Archives

A long-time friend and benefactor of the university, Colgate W. Darden, Jr., was commencement speaker June 8, 1969. A former governor of Virginia, Darden contributed greatly to the university and to the School of Education which bears his name. He was a recipient of the University Medal which is the highest recognition awarded by the university. Courtesy of University Archives

Earl Thomas Gresham was a member of the first Advisory Board which Lewis W. Webb, Jr., appointed after becoming director of the Norfolk Division in 1946. He was a particularly good friend of the library, in which he was pictured here. A recipient of Norfolk's First Citizen Award, Gresham played a key role in helping to establish the library on a sound financial footing in the 1960s, at what was a critical juncture in the school's development. Gresham Hall dormitory was named for E. T. Gresham. Courtesy of Mrs. E. G. Chilton

Warren Palmer, left, president of the Exchange Club of Norfolk, Lewis W. Webb, Jr., and Virginia First District Congressman Thomas N. Downing strolled through American history as they viewed twenty-eight reproductions of significant documents from the nation's past. The Freedom Shrine was dedicated February 22, 1965, in the assembly hall of the Hughes Library. Downing, who was from Newport News, served on the independent college's first Board of Visitors. Courtesy of University Archives

Governor Linwood Holton visited the sixty-five-foot research vessel which he, Congressman G. William Whitehurst, and Admiral Elmo Zumwalt secured for the university from the Coast Guard. Christened on Columbus Day, October 12, 1971, the ship has played an important part in the university's emphasis on oceanography. Courtesy of Public Information Services

From left to right, Bruce Bishop, student body president and later secretary of the Board of Visitors, and board members Francis N. Crenshaw, Rev. Milton A. Reid, Dorothy Doumar, Edgar S. Everhart, and university Vice President Harold Eickhoff watched an oceanography demonstration by department chairman John Ludwig during a campus tour. Crenshaw, Everhart, and Doumar served as the second, third, and fourth rectors of the board, respectively. Bishop, a graduate of the class of 1973, was honored with the Distinguished Alumni Award in 1981. Courtesy of University Archives; photograph by Peter Harahan

J. M. Piette, vice president and general manager of the Union Camp Corporation of Franklin, Virginia, on the left; Senator William B. Spong, Jr., of Portsmouth, center; and university President James L. Bugg, Jr., talked together following Union Camp's contribution of funds in support of groundwater hydrology research at the university.

In 1985, Union Camp also donated to the university, through The Nature Conservancy, 318 acres of forest land on the Blackwater River valued at $508,000. The Old Dominion University Blackwater Ecologic Preserve in Isle of Wight County contains several rare species of trees as well as other flora and fauna. Lytton J. Musselman of the biology department played a key role in the university's acquisition of this valuable natural, living laboratory. Courtesy of University Archives

University benefactors Reid M. Spencer, George M. Kaufman, Henry Clay Hofheimer II, and Roy B. Martin, Jr., left to right, enjoyed a light-hearted moment at the home of the president. Courtesy of University Archives; photograph by John Servais

Seated with university President Alfred B. Rollins, Jr., center, were, left to right, Virginia legislators L. Cleaves Manning ('46), Owen B. Pickett, Thomas W. Moss, Jr., and Stanley C. Walker, who visited the campus to pledge their continued support for university funding. Walker has not only been a strong supporter of the university in the Senate of Virginia but has also donated his political papers to the University Archives. Manning received the Distinguished Alumni Award in 1985. Courtesy of Public Information Services

Rector Francis N. Crenshaw recognized John R. Sears, Jr., upon his retirement from the Board of Visitors. Among his contributions to the university, Sears served as vice rector of the Board. Courtesy of University Archives; photograph by Steve Shires

Richard Bagley of Hampton, chairman of the House of Delegates' Appropriations Committee, visited the campus in 1978 with the governor's capital outlay tour. He was among a group of state legislators who worked hard to secure funding for the university. Courtesy of Public Information Services

John H. Dorroh, Jr., president of American Business Systems, Inc., left, demonstrated one of the computers which he donated to the School of Business and Public Administration in 1986. Gail Mullin, the dean of the school, center, and Vice President David T. Shufflebarger, right, listened intently to learn about the equipment which was valued at more than $100,000. Courtesy of Public Information Services

M. Lee Payne served as rector of the Board of Visitors from 1982 until 1984. Courtesy of Public Information Services

Harry H. Mansbach, right, was surprised at his office when Bernie Kirsch, president of the Alumni Association, presented him with the Honorary Alumnus Award in 1986. A recipient of the University Medal for his contributions to the university, Mansbach served on the Educational Foundation and the President's Council. Courtesy of Public Information Services

Virginia Beach real estate developer R. G. Moore, a major financial contributor and an ardent supporter of the university's athletic program, became a member of the Board of Visitors in 1986. Courtesy of Public Information Services

Bernie Kirsch, president of the Alumni Association, presented the Honorary Alumnus Award to Gene Walters at the August, 1986 Board of Visitors meeting. Walters, president of Farm Fresh, Inc., served on the Board of Visitors, where he chaired the Advancement Committee. Courtesy of Public Information Services

Lewis W. Webb, Jr.
Director 1946-1957
Provost 1957-1960
President 1960-1969
Courtesy of McIntosh Studio

James L. Bugg, Jr.
President 1969-1976
Courtesy of McIntosh Studio

Alfred B. Rollins, Jr.
President 1976-1985
Courtesy of McIntosh Studio

Joseph M. Marchello
President 1985-
Courtesy of Aufenger Studio

Chapter 3

The Classroom & Community

The university is a marketplace for ideas, the profession of which is the responsibility of the faculty. This objective is accomplished through teaching, research, and public service. In addition, the faculty provides continuity in the life of the institution. The faculty creates the knowledge, transmits the information, and develops the skills which students seek to obtain at the university. The role of the administration and support staff is to facilitate the process by which teachers may teach and conduct research and students may learn what they need to know to make them better human beings and citizens. In this chapter, some of the faculty, administrators, and staff personnel who have dedicated themselves to this effort are featured.

The fall 1930 catalogue announcing classes at the Norfolk Division of the College of William and Mary listed the names of seventeen faculty members and administrators. In 1986, Old Dominion University had 574 full-time tenured faculty members, among whom were 32 who held the prestigious rank of Eminent Professor.

From the very beginning, the Norfolk Division could boast of an excellent faculty drawn from some of the finest universities and colleges in the world. Among the seventeen faculty members and administrators who constituted the first professional staff were educators who held doctorates from such universities as Johns Hopkins, Harvard, Chicago, Radcliffe, Illinois, and Madrid. Some professors commuted from Williamsburg in this period to offer classes at the Norfolk Division. By 1931, additional Ph.D. holders from Johns Hopkins, Harvard, Ohio State, and Heidelberg had been added to the faculty.

Commencing in September, 1931, Virginia Polytechnic Institute also established an affiliation with the Norfolk Division of the College of William and Mary. Just as students were able to complete their first two years of work at the College of William and Mary by attending classes at the Norfolk Division, in 1931 it became possible for students to complete the first two years of the VPI program in engineering by attending classes at the Norfolk Division, thanks to an arrangement agreed upon by President J. A. C. Chandler of William and Mary, and Virginia Tech President Julian A. Burruss. The initiative was probably one of the most innovative and creative undertaken in higher education to that time. Technically, therefore, the college was the Norfolk Division of the College of William and Mary and Virginia Polytechnic Institute. With the VPI connection came a number of "Tech" faculty, and two new instructors, Edward L. White and Lewis W. Webb, Jr., who would have more than a little to do with shaping the destiny of the Norfolk Division. After gaining its independence from the College of William and Mary in February, 1962, the new college also began to lay plans for an engineering school, as a consequence of which Virginia Polytechnic Institute severed its relationship with the new college in September, 1963.

H. Edgar Timmerman was the first director of the Norfolk Division, serving in that capacity from 1930 until 1932. Courtesy of University Archives

Thomas L. Scott, a star athlete at Maury High School in Norfolk and at the Virginia Military Institute, was appointed director of athletics at the Norfolk Division in 1930. Scott coached football, baseball, basketball, and track at the college until his resignation in 1940. During the decade that he coached at the college, "Tommy" Scott was an outstanding role-model and was much beloved. Courtesy of University Archives

In 1932, two new faculty members who would make a profound contribution to the development of the Norfolk Division joined the staff. Edward L. White, on the left in this 1940s picture, and Lewis W. Webb, Jr., both came to the Norfolk Division from Virginia Polytechnic Institute. White taught engineering at the college for forty-two years, including his service as associate dean of the School of Engineering. Webb devoted forty-two years to the institution, including twenty-three years as its chief executive officer. Following his presidency, Webb returned to teaching physics. He retired in 1974. In 1984, he passed away, leaving behind a major university as his legacy to the community he loved. Courtesy of University Archives

Perry Y. Jackson was one of the original faculty members at the Norfolk Division in 1930. Jackson, who held a Ph.D. from the University of Chicago, taught chemistry. He is fondly remembered as a charismatic teacher. Courtesy of University Archives

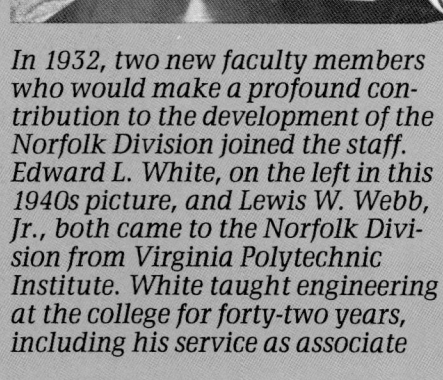

W. Gerald Akers came to the Norfolk Division in 1931 with a Ph.D. from Heidelberg University, Germany. An expert in foreign languages, Akers served on the faculty until his retirement in 1972. Courtesy of University Archives

Edward Gwathmey became the second director of the Norfolk Division in 1932. He held the post only during the last few months of 1932, however, before accepting the presidency of Converse College in South Carolina. Courtesy of University Archives

Robert C. McClelland, professor of history, shown here on the left, with Lewis W. Webb, Jr., in a 1950s vintage photograph, joined the Norfolk Division faculty in 1931. He taught ancient languages at the college until his death in 1962. In addition, McClelland was the college's first historian and the author of Annals of the College of William and Mary in Norfolk, which chronicled the first three decades of the school's history in three volumes. McClelland also served in the administration of the college as director of the evening college. Courtesy of University Archives

Audrey Thomas "Bud" Paul was associated with the Norfolk Division for fourteen years, as proprietor of the lunch counter and bookstore, until his death in 1948. Bud was an enthusiastic booster of the college and is remembered "for his intelligent and understanding heart, for his full measure of devotion to his accepted duty, for his wonderful spirit of beneficence and friendship, for his untiring patience and his depth and thoroughness as a counselor and friend, and for his charm and cheerfulness as a great human being," in the words of Robert E. Giles speaking on behalf of the Student Senate. Prior to the opening of Webb Center, the snack bar-bookstore-student lounge was known as "Bud's Emporium" or simply as "Bud's," in honor of Bud Paul. Courtesy of University Archives

Bessie Charity was well known to most students at the college in the thirties, forties, fifties, and sixties. She first came to the Norfolk Division in 1934. Following the death of Audrey T. "Bud" Paul in 1948, Bessie became manager of the snack bar. She retired in 1969. Courtesy of University Archives

William T. Hodges, who held an Ed.D. from Harvard University, was director of the college from 1933 until 1941. By 1936, faculty members were devoting their full time to teaching at the Norfolk Division, whereas prior to that time a number of faculty commuted back and forth from Williamsburg to Norfolk. Some Norfolk Division faculty also commuted to Williamsburg to present classes at William and Mary as well. Courtesy of University Archives

Charles J. Duke served as director of the Norfolk Division from 1941 to 1946. It was during his term of office that the college first began receiving annual appropriations from the state. Courtesy of University Archives

This 1942 photograph is one of the earliest group faculty pictures which survives. Seated in the first row, from left to right, were David S. Prosser, Lewis W. Webb, Jr., Sarah Rogers, Flossie Ratcliffe, Dorothy Pierce Newby, Dorothy Lucker, E. Ruffin Jones, and Ernest Gray. In the second row, left to right, were Donald Gordon, David Camp, Edward L. White, Frank A. MacDonald, W. Gerald Akers, Lee M. Klinefelter, Robert Luce, and John Haywood.

Webb, White, and Klinefelter were involved in the college's program of war training courses and vocational education at the time. Prosser, who taught business and economics, Gray, who taught English, and E. Ruffin Jones, who taught biology, had all come to the Norfolk Division by 1931. Prosser remained at the college until 1944, Jones until 1946, and Gray until 1947. Many former students will no doubt also recall taking classes in philosophy with Frank MacDonald before he left the Norfolk Division and became chairman of the philosophy department at William and Mary. Newby was the college librarian. Lucker taught English, and Ratcliffe taught secretarial science. Courtesy of University Archives

48

In 1954, the fine arts faculty included, left to right, Herbert L. Sebren, Violet K. S. Breneiser, Rogers D. Whichard, W. Gerald Akers who was department chairman, S. Eliot Breneiser, Charles E. Vogan, and Harold G. Hawn. Whichard was on the faculty from 1948 until his retirement in 1972. Vogan served on the faculty from 1950 until his retirement in 1976. Hawn has been a member of the music faculty since 1953. S. Eliot Breneiser came to the Norfolk Division in 1951 and taught in the music department until his retirement in 1986, subsequent to which he was honored with the Honorary Alumnus Award. Breneiser's wife, Violet K. S. Breneiser, also came to the Norfolk Division in 1951. She taught in the Department of Foreign Languages until her retirement in 1986. Herbert L. Sebren was band director for a number of years and served in the English department. He has been a member of the university faculty since 1946. Courtesy of University Archives

The English department in 1954 included the following faculty members, seated, from left to right, Marcia R. Lindemann, William W. Seward, Jr., who was department chairman, and Mildred Peele; and, standing, from left to right, Reuben Cooper, John Benson, Herbert L. Sebren, and James B. Reece. Seward was on the faculty from 1945 until his retirement in 1977, and was a friend of novelist Ernest Hemingway. Cooper taught at the university from 1946 until his retirement in 1976. Reece, who retired in 1981, joined the faculty in 1952. Courtesy of University Archives

The 1954 mathematics department included the following faculty members, from left to right, Lermond H. Miller, Jeanette F. Whitehurst, Margaret C. Phillips, and Edward T. Hodges. Phillips taught at the university from 1943 until her retirement in 1979. Courtesy of University Archives

This 1954 picture shows, left to right, William M. Beck, Jr., Wallis Gearing, Edward L. White, who was department chairman, and Yates Stirling III of the engineering department. Beck taught at the university from 1946 until his retirement in 1979. Stirling was on the faculty from 1948 until his retirement in 1972. Courtesy of University Archives

Included among the faculty of the Department of Business Administration in 1954 were, from left to right, Dorothy M. Jones, Vance E. Grover, Everette N. Hong, who was department chairman, Myrtle E. Callahan, R. C. Burton, and John R. Willsey. Jones taught at the university from 1954 until her retirement in 1976, and Grover taught at the university from 1946 until his retirement in 1975. Courtesy of University Archives

The science department included the following faculty members in 1954, standing, from left to right, Parker Baum, Donald K. Marchand, Jr., and Jean E. Pugh; and, seated, from left to right, Calder S. Sherwood III, who was department chairman, Kenneth A. Wagner, and Virginia S. Bagley. Marchand, who has both taught and served in the administration of the university as dean of Student Affairs, has been a member of the faculty since 1954. Sherwood was on the university faculty from 1939 until his retirement in 1977. Bagley retired from the university in 1985, having joined the faculty in 1945. Courtesy of University Archives

Members of the 1954 physical education department, pictured from left to right, were Arthur B. "Bud" Metheny, Emily Pittman, and Joseph C. "Scrap" Chandler, who was chairman. Metheny taught at the university from 1948 until his retirement in 1980. In addition to coaching baseball and basketball, he also served as director of athletics for several years. Pittman taught at the university from 1950 until her retirement in 1976. Chandler, who coached track and swimming, was on the faculty from 1942 until his retirement in 1969. Courtesy of University Archives

The pay of college professors was not everything it should have been in the 1950s, and as a consequence some young professors supplemented their pay by working at summer jobs which were very different from their academic careers. This young history professor, G. William Whitehurst, was featured in a story in the Norfolk Ledger-Dispatch in the summer of 1955 as he made his way around Tidewater selling Fuller Brushes. It is not known how well he did selling brushes, but it is known that he went on to bigger and better things.

After serving in the Department of History, Whitehurst served in the college's administration for several years as dean of men and then as dean of students. In 1968, he was elected to represent the Second Congressional District of Virginia in the U.S. House of Representatives, a post in which he served with distinction until his retirement in 1986. Whitehurst's "retirement" plans called for him to return to teaching at Old Dominion University, where his students will no doubt benefit from his many years of experience in national and international affairs. *Courtesy of University Archives; photograph by J. D. Klebau*

Shown in this 1954 photograph were William C. Pollard, the college librarian, on the left, and T. Ross Fink, who was chairman of the elementary education department. Fink, who was at the university from 1954 until his retirement in 1970, also served as dean of the Darden School of Education. *Courtesy of University Archives*

Shown studying one of his works in progress in this 1956 photograph was Charles K. Sibley of the art department. Sibley, who became chairman of the department in 1955 retired in 1980 after twenty-five years at the university. He is one of the best known artists in the state. *Courtesy of University Archives*

51

Rebecca O. White, shown here at a 1964 function, served as dean of women in the 1950s and 1960s. Courtesy of University Archives

Raymond L. Quirk, Jr., president of the Imps Fraternity, on the left, offered retired Admiral Harold J. Wright the formal guest book on the occasion of the opening of the Imps Fraternity House in the fall of 1956. Wright, who was the college's admissions officer at the time, also served in other administrative posts and taught classes in the philosophy department. Quirk returned to the college following his graduation and served for a number of years as comptroller and business manager of the university before going into private business. Courtesy of University Archives

W. Herman Bell was a familiar figure on campus and was known to many who sought his advice and assistance as a friendly and sympathetic director of counselling. He served at the university from 1957 until his retirement in 1970. Courtesy of University Archives; photograph by Thomas Thomas

Stanley R. Pliska, who was head of the social studies division of the college when this 1958 picture was taken, conducted a television class in world geography during the 1957-1958 school year. The Norfolk Division thus became the first college in the state to institute a program of televised courses for college credit.

Pliska served at the university from 1946 until his retirement in 1985. In addition to serving as chairman of the history department, Pliska also held several administrative posts for a number of years, including the position of dean of General Studies, before returning to teach in the history department before his retirement. Courtesy of University Archives

The Technical Institute, which was established in 1945, was an outgrowth of the vocational and war training program courses offered by the Norfolk Division during World War II. Prior to the development of the junior college system in Virginia and the establishment of a technical-vocational high school in Norfolk, there was no other place for interested students to receive formal training in technical fields.

The importance of the Technical Institute as a component of the college is attested to by this picture of the 1958-1959 faculty of the institute. Seated, left to right, were Emory Rumble, A. I. Godden, E. A. Kovner, L. M. Klinefelter, director of the Technical Institute, B. C. Dickerson, and L. G. Crowder. Standing, left to right, were J. T. Williford, A. L. Cordell, William O'Brien, J. Tusinski, L. A. Hobbs, E. W. Steele, W. T. James, Jr., G. T. Rodeheaver, S. W. Mauck, W. G. Pogue, J. S. Fitzgerald, W. H. Thornton, and Don McGee. Courtesy of University Archives

Marceline G. Staples served as veterans' advisor at the university between 1948 and her retirement in 1965. Her daughter, Marceline Staples, would later serve the university for over thirty years. Courtesy of University Archives

M. Marceline Staples followed in her mother's footsteps in her service and devotion to the university. Joining the staff in 1952, she served for ten years in the office of finance. She then served as director of records and registration from 1973 until 1981, retiring from the university in 1983. She is shown here with retired Admiral William E. Howard, Jr., in the center, who was director of admissions and registration at the time, and with Grady H. Wicker, on the right, who was director of counselling. Courtesy of University Archives

Tracy B. Nabers, on the left, shown here discussing a problem in mechanical engineering technology, has been a member of the faculty since 1962. Courtesy of University Archives

Jacques Zaneveld of the oceanography department, shown here in the center, planted the flag of the Old Dominion College oceanographic laboratory in Antarctica during a 1964-1965 expedition to the bottom of the world. Accompanying Zaneveld were students Jim Curtis, on the left, and Jack Fletcher. Zaneveld taught at the university from 1959 to 1975. Two of his sons are numbered among the university's alumni. Courtesy of University Archives

Reference Librarian Benjamin F. Clymer, Jr., was on the university faculty from 1960 until his retirement in 1981, following which he continued to serve in the university's advancement office. Clymer was also a generous benefactor of the library, having made a substantial retirement gift to the reference department. Courtesy of University Archives

By 1965 the art department had grown considerably, and included a number of very talented artists and teachers. Seated in the foreground was Charles K. Sibley. Seated behind Sibley, from left to right, were Victor A. Pickett, Florence Zetlin, Marjory Strauss, and Evelyn Dreyer. Standing, from left to right, were Kenneth G. Daley, Alice Jaffe, Parker Lesley, Ernest Mauer, and Suzanne Seel. Courtesy of University Archives

Andrew C. Tunyogi served on the faculty from 1958 until his retirement in 1973. Tunyogi, who was chairman of the philosophy department, was photographed here emerging from the old barracks-style structure known as the Social Studies Building, which was demolished in 1971. Courtesy of University Archives

This "flower child" of the 1960s was none other than the distinguished professor of political science Robert L. Stern. The occasion was the annual "Faculty Frolics" of 1968. Stern taught at the university from 1945 until his retirement in 1978. Stern, who was devoted to the university, died February 2, 1987. It is a tribute to his memory, his wit, and his sense of humor, that no one would have enjoyed this picture more than he. Courtesy of University Archives

John W. Ramsey of the Department of Political Science and Geography has been a strong advocate for the faculty. An active member of the Faculty Senate over the years, he is also an ardent supporter of the American Association of University Professors, which is the principal professional organization representing faculty interests. Courtesy of Public Information Services; photograph by Jay Laundre

Two important women in the life of President Lewis W. Webb, Jr., were, on the right, "First Lady" of the University, Virginia Webb, the president's wife, and, on the left, Norma Hamilton, the president's executive secretary for many years. The picture was taken at a staff Christmas luncheon in 1968. Courtesy of University Archives; photograph by Associated Visual Arts Studio

Alex B. Jackson was one of the most celebrated members of the university's art department in the 1970s. Jackson, the first full-time black faculty member on the university staff, was a member of the faculty from 1967 until his death in March, 1981. Courtesy of University Archives

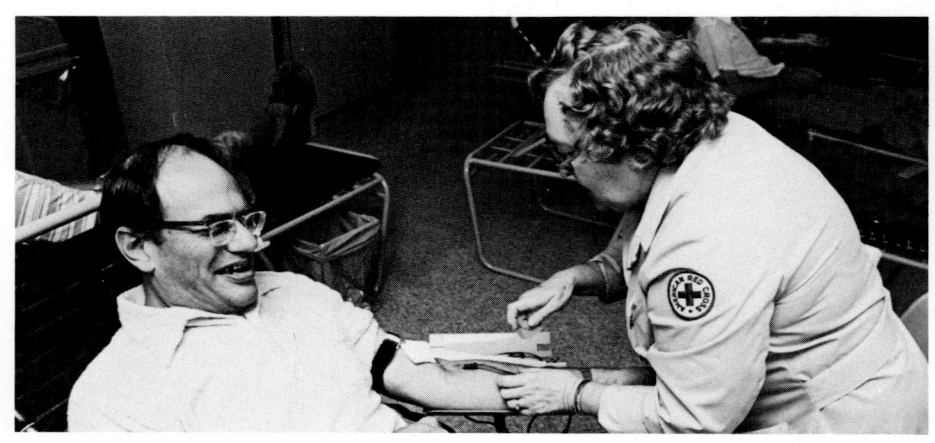

Edgar A. Kovner, professor of mechanical engineering technology and associate dean of engineering, was one of many university faculty, staff members, and students who supported Red Cross blood drives on campus over the years. Courtesy of University Archives

Melvin A. Pittman, who was dean of sciences, was at the university from 1967 to 1974. Courtesy of University Archives

In a light-hearted display of enthusiasm, Katherine Haggarty, on the left, and Annabel Sacks of the Darden School of Education demonstrated that teaching can be fun. Sacks was director of student teaching. Courtesy of University Archives; photograph by John Paradise

President Alfred B. Rollins, Jr., on the right, presented Charles Tanner with a silver pitcher on the occasion of his retirement in 1982 following twelve years of service to the university. Courtesy of Public Information Services; photograph by Jay Laundre

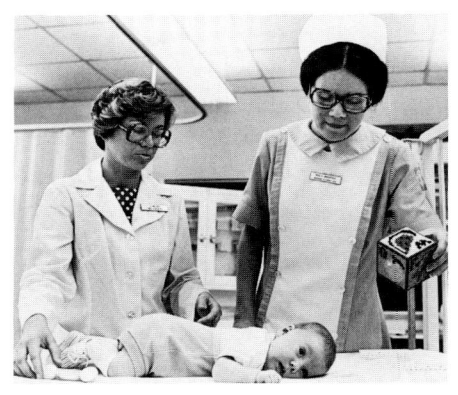

The School of Sciences and Health Professions trains professionals to serve the region and the nation. In this photograph, Joyce E. Miller of the nursing department, on the left, was shown instructing nursing student S. Brassfield in providing care for a new resident of the area. Courtesy of Public Information Services

A practical application of faculty research for the community is shown in the hydraulic model of the Lafayette River which was set up in a Duckworth Memorial Hall laboratory. Chin Y. Kuo, on the left, was shown here supervising a graduate and an undergraduate student in civil engineering. Courtesy of Public Information Services

Clifford L. Adams, who was on the faculty from 1958 until his retirement in 1979, took part in the 1977 signing of the charter of the Old Dominion University chapter of the Phi Kappa Phi honor society. Watching the signing, on the right, was Ben Butler Morgan, Jr., of the psychology department. Courtesy of University Archives

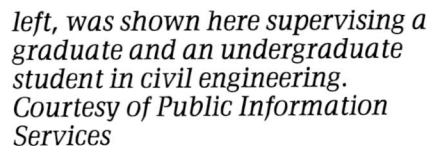

Charles O. Burgess, vice president for academic affairs, on the right, presented the NASA Certificate of Recognition to Norman V. Cohen in March, 1978. The award is one of many grants, contracts, and awards which testify to the close working relationship between the School of Engineering and the National Aeronautics and Space Administration. Courtesy of University Archives

57

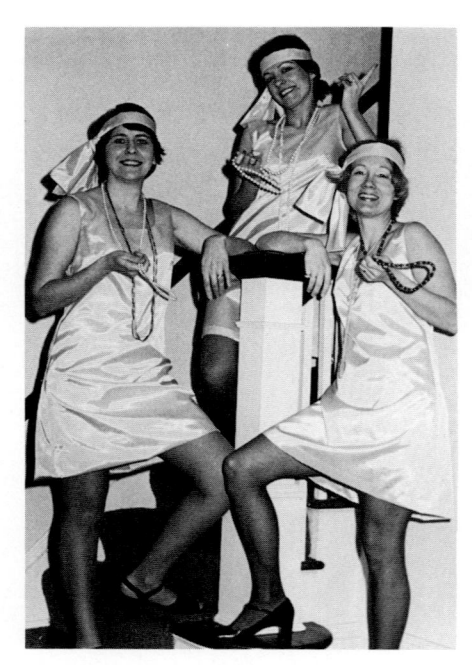

The Faculty Wives Club often provided moments of merriment in the sometimes somber halls of ivy, metaphorically speaking. The "flappers" shown here in a nostalgic and naughty pose were, from left to right, Ann Henry, Audrey Richardson, and Linda Kuehl. Courtesy of University Archives; photograph by Jay Laundre

Old Dominion University has an active Women's Center. Shown here, in 1979, from left to right, were three of the campus leaders behind the center: Nancy T. Bazin, the first director of the women's studies program at the university; Julie White, director of the Women's Center; and Carolyn H. Rhodes of the English department. Courtesy of Public Information Services

Juliet D. Sears served the university for a number of years as the staff member with the responsibility for scheduling rooms and events. Courtesy of University Archives

In 1981, Dean Ulysses V. Spiva of the Darden School of Education, on the left, and A. Rufus Tonelson ('32), special assistant to the president, on the right, presented Norfolk Public School Superintendent Albert L. Ayars with an award for outstanding leadership in the field of education. Courtesy of Public Information Services

This photograph was taken at a luncheon for Faculty Emeriti in February, 1982. From left to right, with years of service in parentheses, those pictured were, Ernest L. Rhodes (1960-1980), who is only partially visible; William H. Patterson (1961-1981); Edward L. White (1932-1974); Arthur C. Munyan (1961-1973); Dorothy Mae Jones (1954-1976); Louis G. Plummer (1956-1975); Clifford L. Adams (1958-1979); Dean E. Vernon Peele (1948-1975); Ruth F. Harrell (1955-1970), who was standing in front of Peele; W. Gerald Akers (1931-1972), who was standing behind Peele; Thomas Blossom (1964-1977); Eminent Professor E. Grant Meade (1965-1979), who was standing behind Blossom; Margaret C. Phillips (1943-1979), who was standing in front of Blossom; M. Lee Klinefelter (1942-1959); David E. Henderson (1965-1981), who was standing behind Klinefelter; Andrew C. Tunyogi (1958-1973), who was standing next to Phillips; W. Herman Bell (1957-1970); Yates Stirling III (1948-1972); and, William E. Hopkins (1962-1980). Courtesy of Public Information Services

The Mary Denson Pretlow Planetarium, which is situated next to the John S. Alfriend Chemistry Building, is one of the many university facilities which serves the regional population directly. On this occasion, Donald B. Hanna, astronomy professor and director of the planetarium, was speaking to a large group of young school children. Courtesy of Public Information Services

The Old Dominion University Faculty Trio is well known throughout the community for its excellent musical presentations. The members of the trio shown here are, from left to right, Gordon Baughman on violin, Harold J. Protsman on piano, and Janet Kriner on cello. Courtesy of Public Information Services

Norval R. Stanaway is regarded by many faculty members and administrators as one of the university's most valuable assets. As assistant director of dining operations, Stanaway is responsible for arranging the banquets and luncheons which the university sponsors on special occasions. Courtesy of Public Information Services

The School of Business Administration conducts practical as well as theoretical research for the community. James A. Pope III of the Department of Management Information Systems and Decision Sciences, on the left; Mark L. Chadwin of the management department, in the foreground; and Wayne K. Talley of the economics department, on the right, were shown here collaborating in a study conducted at the Norfolk International Terminals. Also shown is Joy Moses, a research assistant on the project. Courtesy of Public Information Services

Faculty research benefits the community in very practical ways. In the School of Sciences, professionals work to understand and to preserve the environment. Lytton J. Musselman of the biology department, shown here, studies plants in the university's Blackwater Ecologic Preserve. The property, given to the university by Union Camp Corporation, illustrates the fruitful partnership which business and the university have undertaken in furthering the well-being of the citizens of the region. Courtesy of Public Information Services

Stephanie Marson-Brothers, president of the Hourly and Classified Employees (HACE) organization, presented an honorary membership in the organization to President Alfred B. Rollins, Jr., at the HACE luncheon in May, 1985, in recognition of the president's support of the group. Shown on the right was Matthew A. Krakower, assistant vice president for support services. Courtesy of University Archives

Joseph M. Marchello's inauguration as the university's fourth president, in the fall of 1985, brought together an impressive array of platform dignitaries. At the rostrum in this picture was William Eisenbeiss ('64), president of the Alumni Association. Seated, from left to right in the foreground, were President Alfred B. Rollins, Jr., President Marchello, Governor Charles S. Robb, Robert M. Stanton ('61), rector of the Board of Visitors, and, President James L. Bugg, Jr. Courtesy of Herbert L. Sebren

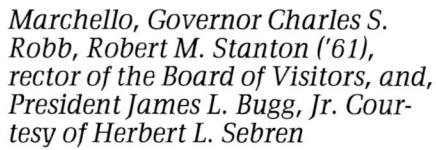

President Joseph M. Marchello, on the left, and Hassan Mekouar, the dean of the Faculty of Letters at Mohammed V University in Rabat, Morocco, in the center, are shown here signing the contract which established a faculty exchange program between the two universities in 1985. Seated at the right is Charles O. Burgess, dean of the School of Arts and Letters. Under the agreement, Old Dominion professors teach in Morocco, and Moroccan professors regularly teach at Old Dominion. International Programs became an area of major emphasis for the university in the late 1970s, as the university broadened its perspective on the community it serves. Courtesy of Public Information Services

President Joseph M. Marchello is seen in this photograph operating one of the computer terminals in the university library. Assisting him is Cynthia B. Duncan, the dean of library services and administration. Courtesy of Public Information Services

Heinz K. Meier of the history department succeeded E. Vernon Peele as dean of the School of Arts and Letters in July, 1975, and served in that position until July, 1985. Meier has been a member of the university faculty since 1960. Courtesy of University Archives

61

Charles M. DeHority taught in the Department of Business Management at the university from 1966 until his retirement in 1986. He also served for a number of years as director of graduate studies in business and economics. Courtesy of University Archives

There were several hourly and classified employees on the staff in 1986 who had served the university twenty-five years or more. This picture features three of those employees. James Bailey, on the left, was a painter with twenty-seven years of service. Mary Wilridge, in the center, was a custodial worker with twenty-seven years of service. Willie Blondino, on the right, the buildings and grounds supervisor, had twenty-six years of service. Courtesy of Public Information Services; photograph by Robert Firek

Edna Wade was a clerk in dining operations in 1986. She had twenty-six years of service to the university as of that date. Courtesy of Public Information Services; photograph by Robert Firek

Chief engineer for NASA's Viking Program, Israel Taback received an honorary doctorate at the May, 1986 graduation ceremonies. The university marked the tenth anniversary of the program which landed the first two spacecraft on the surface of Mars. Taback was technical head of the Mars missions and designed the Lunar Orbiter spacecraft. Ernest Cross, dean of the School of Engineering, hooded Taback as rector of the Board of Visitors Robert M. Stanton, left, and university President Joseph M. Marchello, right, looked on. Courtesy of Public Information Services

Operated by Old Dominion University, the Virginia Center for World Trade offers non-credit courses and information services for the region and state in the area of international trade. The first programs began in May, 1984. Governor Charles S. Robb, on the right, officially opened the center in September, 1984. Shown with the governor were Robert Bray of the Virginia Port Authority, on the left, and Robert M. Stanton, rector of the Old Dominion University Board of Visitors, in the center. Courtesy of Public Information Services

The attractive new offices of the Virginia Center for World Trade are located in this modern building which is located at the Waterside in downtown Norfolk. Courtesy of Public Information Services

Governor Gerald L. Baliles, at the podium, opened the new headquarters of the center in October, 1986. With the governor was Richard Davis, former lieutenant governor of the commonwealth, who was named director of the center in April, 1986. Courtesy of Public Information Services

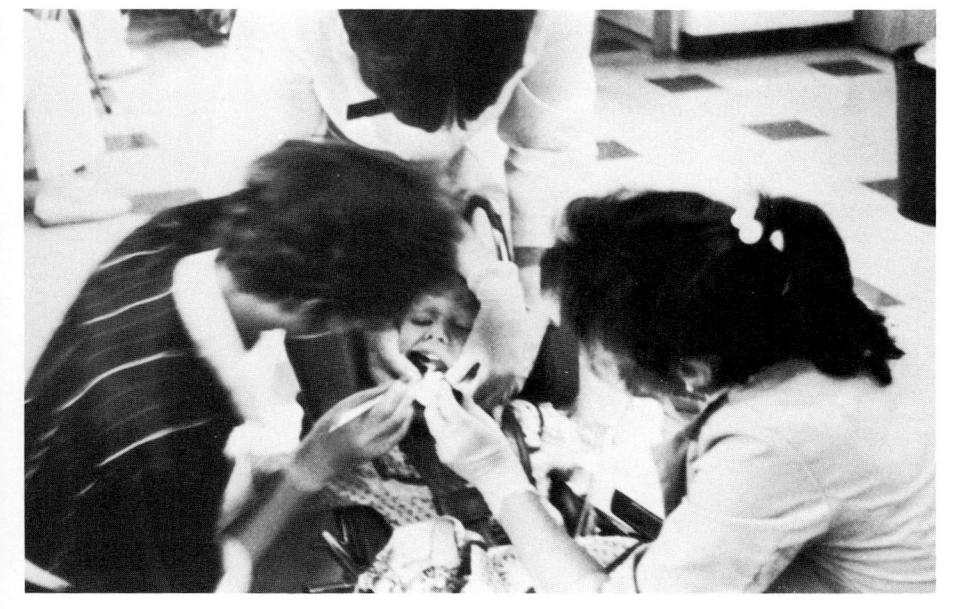

The dental hygiene clinic is an outstanding facility for community service. Here one of the children of the community received care. Courtesy of Public Information Services; photograph by Center for Instructional Development

Michelle M. Darby, Eminent Professor and chairwoman of the dental hygiene department, and Gene W. Hirschfeld, Eminent Professor Emeritus of dental hygiene, who developed the university's dental hygiene program to a level of national prominence, are shown here in the campus facility which was opened in September, 1968 under the sponsorship of the Virginia Tidewater Dental Association Foundation. Courtesy of Public Information Services

In 1986, a number of current faculty members who had served twenty-five years or more at the university came together for a picture session. They are represented in the following six photographs. Others on the 1986 faculty who had served twenty-five years or more at the university, but who were unable to attend the picture session, were Elizabeth C. Guy, Alex Hawryluk, James O. Henry, Jr., Alf J. Mapp, Jr., Heinz K. Meier, Allan Owen, Leland D. Peterson, John R. Richardson, Jr., Thomas M. "Pete" Robinson, Kehar S. Sangha, Stephen P. Shao, Daniel E. Sonenshine, Daniel S. Wilson, Jack H. Wilson. Courtesy of Public Information Services

From the School of Education were Beverley B. Johnson, on the left, and Natalie W. Etheridge.

From the School of Sciences and Health Professions were, reading left to right, Forrest P. "Pat" Clay, Jr., Donald K. Marchand, Jr., Cephas J. Adkins, Jr., James L. Hatfield, and Allen K. Clark.

From the School of Engineering were, reading left to right, Leonard A. Hobbs, J. Hirst Lederle, William H. Thornton, and Raymond E. Ferrari.

From the School of Arts and Letters seated from left to right, were Dorothy E. Johnson and Elizabeth G. Pappas, and standing left to right, Robert F. Young and Harold G. Hawn.

From the School of Business were, standing, John R. Tabb, and seated from left to right, Max B. Jones, Anne S. Daughtrey, and Albert Teich, Jr.

From the Department of English and the School of Arts and Letters were, seated from left to right, Margaret Hay Daugherty and Conrad S. Festa, and standing left to right, Herbert L. Sebren, Roy E. Aycock, and Charles O. Burgess. Burgess was dean of the School of Arts and Letters and Festa was associate dean of the school.

The Alumni Association established the A. Rufus Tonelson Award in 1978 in honor of one of the university's most beloved alumni. The award is given annually to a faculty member in recognition of his or her "devotion to excellence and significant contributions to both the welfare of the community and the stature of Old Dominion University through teaching, research and service." In 1978, three faculty members shared the award: Richard Tersine, Patricia S. Moschel, and Louis H. Henry. Some of the award winners are pictured below.

Louis H. Henry of the economics department was honored in 1978. Courtesy of Public Information Services

Charles H. Haws of the history department was honored in 1979. Courtesy of Public Information Services

S. Eliot Breneiser of the music department was honored in 1980. Courtesy of Public Information Services

Kenneth G. Daley of the art department was honored in 1981. Courtesy of Public Information Services

John A. Fahey of the foreign languages department was honored in 1982. Courtesy of Public Information Services

Daniel E. Sonenshine of the biology department was honored in 1983. Courtesy of University Archives

Gennaro L. Goglia of the mechanical engineering and mechanics department was also honored in 1983. Courtesy of Public Information Services

Katherine C. Kersey of the child study and special education department was honored in 1984. Courtesy of Public Information Services; photograph by Rochefort Photography

Raymond H. Kirby of the psychology department was honored in 1985. Courtesy of Public Information Services

Harold G. Marshall of the biology department was honored in 1986. Courtesy of University Archives

Gordon A. McDougall, a graduate of the class of 1980, became director of the Alumni Association in May, 1982. During his student days, McDougall served as president of the student body, chairman of the honor council, and as student representative to the Board of Visitors. In his present capacity, he also serves as secretary to the Board of Visitors. Courtesy of Public Information Services

In 1986, a number of the past presidents of the Alumni Association gathered on campus for a meeting. Pictured here, from left to right, with the years they served as president, are W. Frank Latham, Jr., ('56) 1963-1964, Gene A. Woolard ('68) 1980-1982, Donald J. Porter ('64) 1969-1971, William I. Foster, Jr., ('60) 1967-1969, T. Earl Nettles ('59) 1960-1961, Thomas A. Perry ('64) 1984-1985, Shannon T. Mason, Jr., ('59) 1964-1965, William Eisenbeiss ('64) 1985-1986, Donald G. Griffin ('38) 1946-1956, Robert L. Fodrey, Sr., ('57) 1958-1960, Albert B. Gornto, Jr., ('56) 1961-1962, Roger L. Frost ('61) 1971-1973, George C. Winslow ('66) 1975-1977, Douglas L. Roberts ('56) 1956-1957, and F. Bernard Kirsch III, ('64) 1986-1987. Past Alumni Association presidents not pictured include James K. Hall ('57) 1982-1984, Ray W. Dezern, Jr., ('67) 1977-1980, H. Mercer Davis ('65) 1973-1975, Donald E. Wirt ('60) 1966-1967, Jack W. Mace ('61) 1965-1966, Archie T. Bruns ('58) 1962-1963, and Kenneth E. Brown ('57) 1957-1958. Courtesy of Public Information Services

Margaret B. Holland, assistant director of alumni relations, first came to the alumni office in 1963 as part-time secretary of the Alumni Association. She was the second person to hold that position, the first having been Elizabeth T. Spencer. During her tenure she has witnessed the growth of the Alumni Association to approximately forty thousand university graduates. Courtesy of Public Information Services; photograph by Michael Blanton

Chapter 4

Distinguished Alumni

Old Dominion University is a young university, one which has more of a future than a past. Founded in 1930 as a branch of the College of William and Mary, the college graduated its first four-year class in 1956. There were fifteen graduates in that class. In 1985-1986, the university conferred a total of 2,441 degrees, including 24 doctorates, 15 certificates of advanced study, 486 master's degrees, and 1,916 bachelor's degrees. In the thirty years between the awarding of the first four-year degrees and 1986, the university has awarded approximately forty thousand degrees.

The university takes great pride in the thousands of men and women who have passed through its portals on the way to assuming responsible positions of leadership in the community, the state, the nation, and the world. In this chapter, a few of the university's notable alumni have been featured as a representative sample of the many sons and daughters whom the university has helped to develop and of whom it is so proud.

Forrest D. Murden, Jr., ('40) was the recipient of the Distinguished Alumni Award in 1962. An expert on foreign trade and international economics, and most recently president of the consulting firm of Murden and Company of Madison Avenue, New York, Murden had a distinguished career in national affairs and education. In addition to serving as a consultant to the Ford Foundation, United Nations Organization, and the Council for Latin America, among other organizations, Murden also served as an official with such national and international organizations as the Council on Foreign Relations and the American Heritage Foundation. Courtesy of Murden and Company

Mills E. Godwin, Jr., ('32) was honored with the Distinguished Alumni Award in 1963. After serving in the Senate of Virginia, Godwin was elected lieutenant governor in 1961. He was subsequently elected to two terms as governor of Virginia. Courtesy of University Archives

Roy B. Martin, Jr., ('40) was honored with the Distinguished Alumni Award in 1964. Martin, who served many years as a councilman and mayor of the city of Norfolk, has been a good friend of the university. Among his other contributions, he served as a trustee of the Educational Foundation. Courtesy of Public Information Services; photograph by Jay Laundre

Ann H. Kilgore ('42) has made study at Old Dominion University a family affair. Both of her daughters are also alumnae. A councilwoman and mayor of Hampton, Virginia, Kilgore has served on the university's Board of Visitors, the Educational Foundation, and the President's Council. She received the Distinguished Alumni Award in 1965. Courtesy of Public Information Services

Milton B. Ames, Jr., was presented with the Distinguished Alumni Award in 1966. A retired aerospace researcher, Ames has held a number of key positions with NASA, including director of space vehicle research and technology. The recipient of many awards, including two honorary doctorates, Ames has been recognized by NASA with awards for projects Fire, Pegasus, Apollo, X-15, Lifting Bodies, and Space Shuttle. Courtesy of NASA

70

Jack R. Wilkins ('47) was honored with the Distinguished Alumni Award in 1969. A leading Norfolk businessman, Wilkins played a vital role in the establishment of the Intercollegiate Foundation in 1963, and was instrumental in the expansion of the university's athletic programs. He has been a key supporter of the university. Courtesy of Public Information Services

A. Rufus Tonelson ('32) was the recipient of the Distinguished Alumni Award in 1970. Tonelson was a member of the first class at the Norfolk Division in 1930. A basketball player in his student days, Tonelson's love for the game is attested by his many years of service as timekeeper at the Monarchs' home games. A teacher, dean of the School of Education, special assistant to the president for school and community relations, and benefactor of the university, Tonelson retired in 1976. The Tonelson Garden at Webb Center is named in his honor, as is the Tonelson Award, which is presented for outstanding faculty achievement. In 1979, Tonelson was the recipient of the Alumni Association Service Award. Courtesy of University Archives

Henry E. Howell, Jr., ('40) was honored with the Distinguished Alumni Award in 1973. A former member of the Virginia House of Delegates and the Senate of Virginia, Howell was elected to the office of lieutenant governor of Virginia in 1971. A Norfolk attorney, Howell has served on the Alumni Association board of directors. He has also made a significant contribution to scholarship at the university through the donation of his political papers to the University Archives. Courtesy of University Archives; photograph by James Turner

Robert L. Fodrey, Sr., ('57) the 1958-1960 president of the Alumni Association, and Patricia Vincent ('58) discussed plans for the Alumni dance held at the Convention Hall in Virginia Beach in 1959. The dance honored the first three four-year classes to graduate from the Norfolk Division. Fodrey was a recipient of the Distinguished Alumni Award in 1974, and of the Alumni Association Service Award in 1981. Retired from the federal civil service after forty-one years with the U.S. Navy, many of which were spent as director of the Navy's regional office of Civilian Manpower Management in Norfolk, Fodrey has received numerous civilian service awards and distinctions. In 1986, he was awarded the University Medal for his outstanding contributions to the university. Courtesy of University Archives

Alf J. Mapp, Jr., ('61) was honored with the Distinguished Alumni Award in 1982. An Eminent Professor of English, Mapp has been a member of the university faculty since 1961. Courtesy of Public Information Services

Albert B. "Bucky" Gornto, Jr., on the left, was honored by Robert M. Stanton, rector of the Board of Visitors, for his contribution as chairman of the 1983-1984 Annual Fund Campaign for the Educational Foundation. The campaign raised a record $445,000. Gornto, a member of the first four-year class to graduate from the Norfolk Division in 1956, had the distinction of being the first alumnus to serve as vice rector of the Board of Visitors, beginning in 1970. The 1961-1962 president of the Alumni Association and 1979 recipient of the Distinguished Alumni Award, Gornto is one of the top executive officers of Sovran Bank.

Stanton was the first alumnus to serve as rector of the Board of Visitors, having been appointed to the position by the governor in 1984. Stanton is president of Goodman-Segar-Hogan, Inc., a major East Coast commercial real estate property manager and developer. He graduated from the university in 1961. Courtesy of Public Information Services

Samuel Norfleet Etheredge ('33) received the Distinguished Alumni Award in 1984. "Juney" Etheredge, a track star during his student days, was a noted medical doctor and vascular surgeon, now retired. Courtesy of Public Information Services

L. Cleaves Manning ('46) of Portsmouth, Virginia, was honored with the Distinguished Alumni Award in 1985. An attorney and veteran member of the Virginia House of Delegates who was later appointed a judge of the Portsmouth Circuit Court, Manning has been a good friend and supporter of the university. Courtesy of Public Information Services

The April, 1961, alumni dance brought a number of old friends together. From left to right, they were T. Earl Nettles, who was president of the Alumni Association, Jean Holloman, who was dance committee chairman, orchestra leader Tommy Gwaltney, and, Alumni Association board members Donald Will and Robert L. Fodrey, Sr. Holloman was honored with the Alumni Association Service Award in 1980 in recognition of her many years of loyal and enthusiastic support of the university. A member of the Old Dominion University Sports Hall of Fame, Holloman was a member of the first four-year class to graduate from the college in 1956. Courtesy of University Archives

Shannon T. Mason, Jr., ('59) was honored with the Alumni Association Service Award in 1984. "Skip" is a Newport News attorney. He served as president of the Alumni Association in 1964-1965, and as vice rector of the Board of Visitors from 1982 to 1984. Courtesy of Public Information Services

Edgar A. Kovner ('64) received the Alumni Association Service Award in 1982. A member of the university faculty since 1946, Kovner was accorded emeritus faculty status upon his retirement in 1984. Among his teaching and administrative positions was that of dean of the Division of Technology. He and his wife Kathleen are also benefactors of the university, having established a major $75,000 challenge grant to generate scholarship funds for high school students entering the university as freshman engineers. Courtesy of University Archives

Harry S. "Kit" Coffey ('67) received the Alumni Association Service Award in 1983. A retired U.S. Navy commander and aviator, Coffey had served as an active member of the Alumni Association board of directors for ten years at the time of the award. Courtesy of Public Information Services

73

Tommy Newsom ('48) of Portsmouth, Virginia, is a well known television personality and musician. A member of the NBC "Tonight Show" orchestra, Newsom may frequently be seen jousting verbally with "Tonight Show" star Johnny Carson. Aside from his "dead-pan" humor, Newsom is an accomplished musician and leads the orchestra behind "Doc" Severinsen. Newsom, who has been with the orchestra for twenty-three years, returned to the Old Dominion campus in May, 1985, to provide musical entertainment for the graduates of that class and their guests. Newsom's return to campus provided an opportunity for him to hold a reunion with some of his former classmates and band members from the college "swing band" with which he played. That group included Fred Huette, Jr., Linwood Gooding, Alex Runaldue, Frank "Buddy" Wilson, Bob Carr, Lucian Montagna, Bob Reynolds, Buddy Still, Frank Ficarra, John Derieux, and "Ziggy" Harrell. Courtesy of Public Information Services; photograph by Michael Blanton

Two 1959 graduates who represent the achievement of a great many of the students who have graduated from the university are Mary Elizabeth Wheeler and Lawrence C. Lawless. Wheeler, a history graduate, subsequently earned a Ph.D. at the University of North Carolina and taught history at N.C. State. Lawless, who was also a history graduate, earned a law degree from the University of Virginia. Following a number of years of service in the office of the commonwealth's attorney, Lawless became a judge in Norfolk's traffic court. Courtesy of University Archives

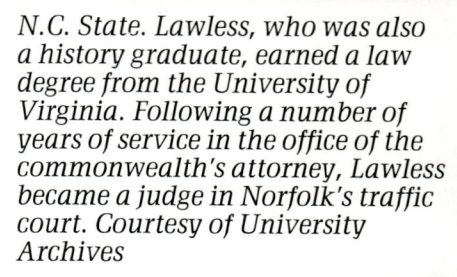

James H. Kabler III, ('69), is a New York real estate developer and businessman. An attorney, Kabler is also a theatrical backer and Broadway producer. Courtesy of Public Information Services

Beth Polson ('73) has won several Emmy Awards for her television productions, among which were some "Barbara Walters Specials," produced for ABC-TV. Polson manages her own independent television production and consulting company in Los Angeles. Courtesy of Public Information Services; photograph by Michael Blanton

The beautiful model and actress Deborah Shelton was a junior at the university in 1970 when she won the Miss U.S.A. title. She was later first runner-up in the Miss Universe pageant. She is shown here with her castmate Larry "J.R." Hagman, the star of the CBS prime-time soap opera "Dallas." Courtesy of Public Information Services

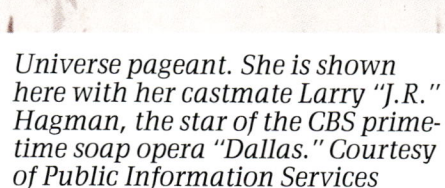

Ronald Fortunato (M.S. '80) was one of 120 finalists in the national teacher-in-space program competition to fly in the space shuttle Challenger. Fortunato teaches in the Norfolk public school system. Courtesy of Public Information Services; photograph by Steve Daniel

Atlanta area alumni who were interested in forming an alumni chapter met in February, 1986, to discuss that possibility. Pictured here were Mark A. Jacobson ('76), standing, and Frank Batkins ('72), on the right. On the left was Mark's wife Rhonda. The number of formally organized alumni chapters was approaching twenty as 1986 drew to a close. Courtesy of Public Information Services; photograph by Steve Daniel

Henry H. Gerber, who received his master's degree in international studies from the university in 1985 at age 78, is believed to be the oldest alumnus ever to earn a degree from Old Dominion University. Gerber is an excellent representative of the "non-traditional" students served by the university. Courtesy of Public Information Services; photograph by Robert Firek

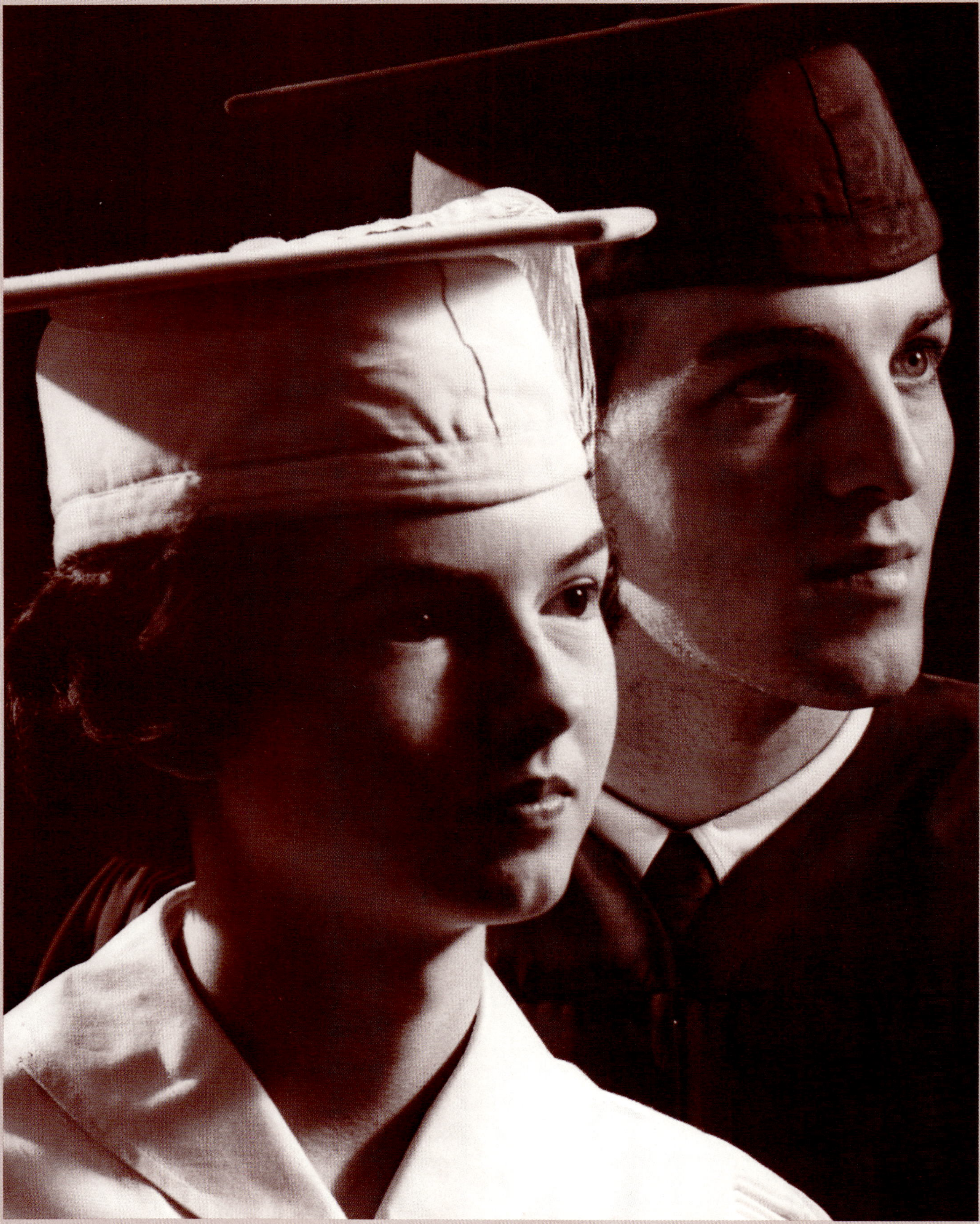

Chapter 5

Student Life

The proud heritage of the institution has enabled students to view new horizons and to overcome difficult challenges. In a most important sense, the university is the students, past and present, who share an important part of their lives on campus.

Student life is reflected not only in what happens in the classroom but also in the rich variety of extracurricular activities and celebrations held each year on the campus. This chapter provides a sketch of some of the activities over the fifty-six year life of the institution. It depicts the classroom, dances, homecoming parades, student government, and the performing arts as well as protest activities and efforts by students to gain support for the university's funding from the state legislature.

The authors hope that this section will help to show the university's commitment to the social and political development of students as well as its concern for the life of the mind and career opportunities. We hope too that former students, present students, and friends of the university will view these pictures and be reminded of many happy occasions from their own experiences at Old Dominion University.

This picture of Carolyn Thomas and Bob Thompson, taken in the mid-1950s, symbolizes the hopes for the future of all students at Old Dominion University. Courtesy of University Archives

ACADEME

An early engineering drawing class at the Norfolk Division of the College of William and Mary and VPI posed for this 1943 photo. Left to right in the front row were I. P. Austin, N. L. Bloxsom, W. H. Wood, M. M. Schaadt and E. L. White, the instructor. In the back row were M. Lomax, W. C. Mochard, A. S. Nelson, J. T. Miller and G. R. Prudew. Courtesy of University Archives; photograph by James C. Brooks

During the 1940s, the Norfolk Division provided extensive training for the Tidewater community as the nation mobilized for World War II. By war's end in 1945, over five thousand people had been schooled in subjects like aircraft mechanics, welding, drafting, electroplating and topographic mapping. Engineering Science Management Defense Training brought naval personnel to the campus to teach. After the war, vocational education flourished so that by the end of the decade, the Technical Institute, created in 1945, was training Tidewater's technicians. The pictures illustrate some of the early activities in the university's partnership with the community which has continued to the present. Courtesy of University Archives

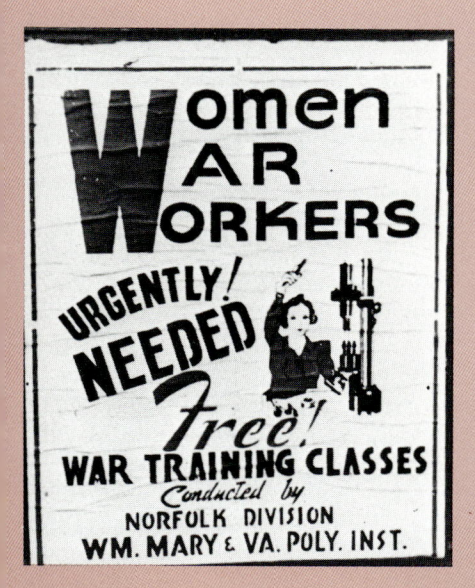

Courtesy of University Archives

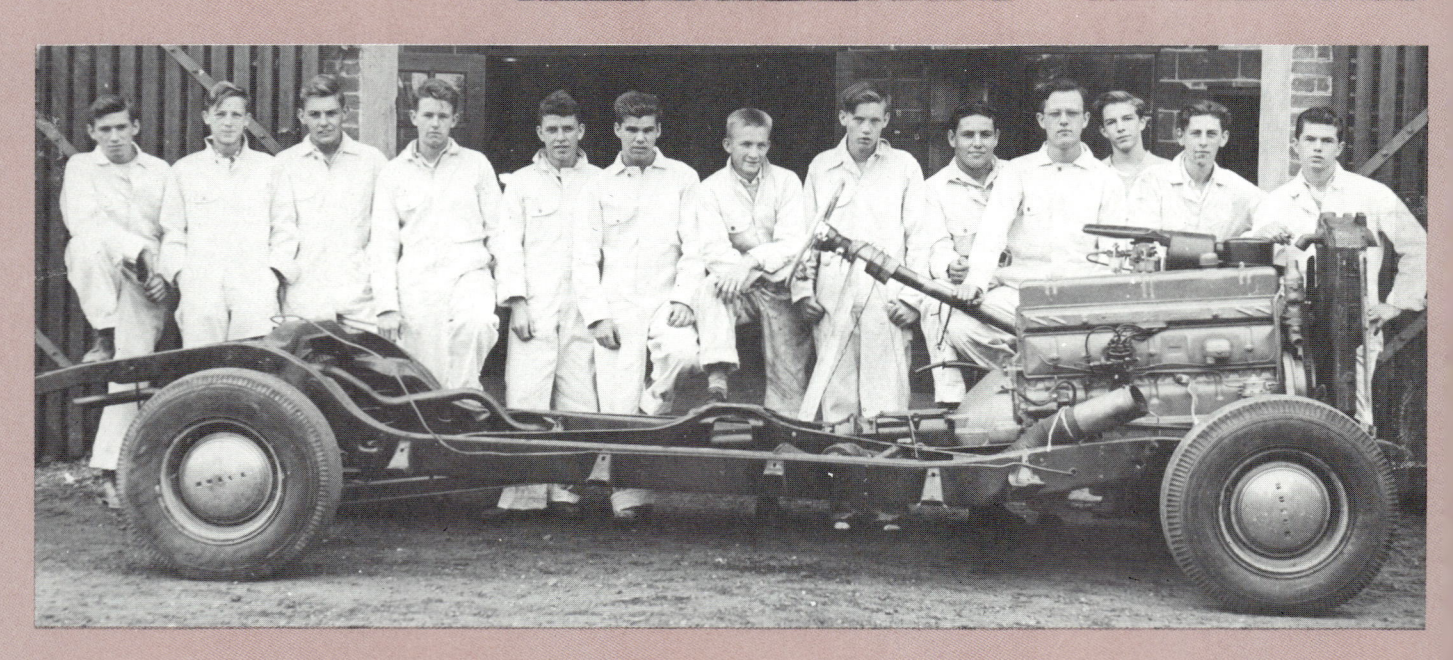

Courtesy of University Archives

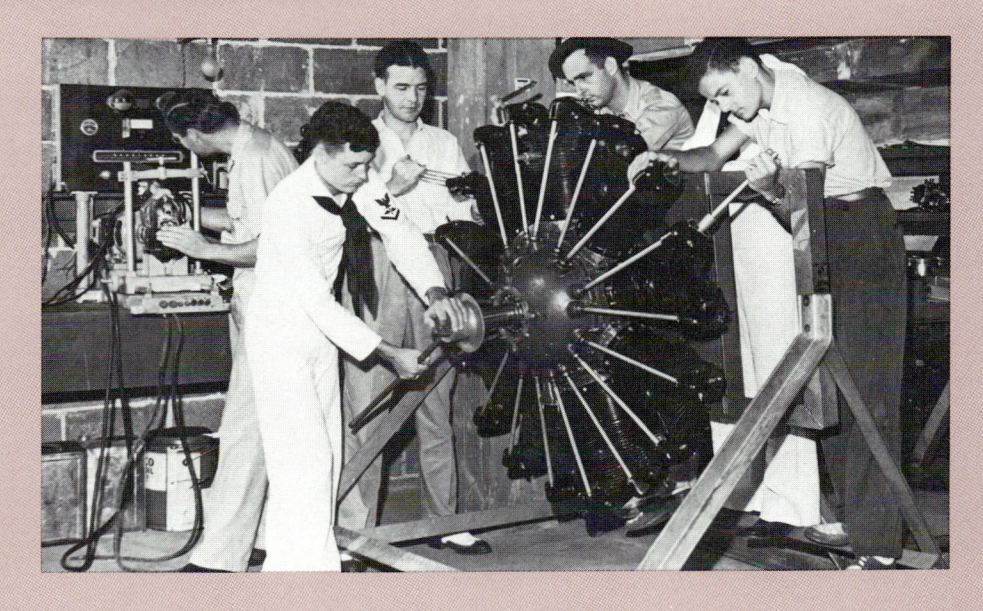

This is an early view of "bookers" in the old Administration Building college library. Courtesy of University Archives

Robert L. Stern's social science class met in the old Larchmont School in the early 1950s. Courtesy of University Archives

Richard Holland of Delta Omega Phi, left, and Lewis Jones of Pi Phi Sigma stacked books during the 1955 drive to collect volumes for the college library. Each hoped that his fraternity would bring in the most books because the prize was a dinner party for the winning team. Courtesy of University Archives

Members of the first four-year graduating class of 1956 were, first row left to right William F. "Frank" Latham, Jr., president, Leigh S. Stewart, Jr., secretary, Jean Leggett Holloman, William Wall, Jr., treasurer, and Robert Latimer, vice president. Second row left to right were Edgar F. Tyree, Jr., Albert B. Gornto, Jr., Kenneth E. Brown, John R. Wikoff, Spyros C. Papachristos, Jesse J. Perry, William Jarrett, Bruce A. Leslie, and Douglas L. Roberts. Not pictured was Joseph Fleischmann. Everett N. Hong, the class sponsor, was at the far right in the second row. Courtesy of University Archives

Medical technology students Eloise Powell, left, and Doris Gautreaux ran quantitative assays for iodine in the blood at the laboratories of Norfolk General Hospital in 1959. Courtesy of University Archives

One of fifteen graduating seniors in 1956, Bruce A. Leslie proofed one of his last exams before getting a B. A. in business administration. Courtesy of University Archives

Phi Theta Kappa, the honorary junior college fraternity and Delta Phi Omega, the honorary senior college fraternity, gathered following Honors Convocation on May 16, 1959. From left to right, front row, were Ruth Snyder, Betty Wheeler, Ann Carruthers, Lois Farwell, Dennis McMurran, Benjamin Blanton, Harold McGee, and Ethel Needham. From left to right, second row, were William Patterson, Mike McDonald, and Frank Burnett. Courtesy of University Archives

Evening students lined up to register in 1959. Long lines have not disappeared yet as shown by the recent photo, in the lower left. Once inside a registration center, below, students studied the boards to determine which classes were open and which had been closed or cancelled. Courtesy of University Archives

85

Robert M. Stanton, current rector of the Board of Visitors, received his diploma from President Lewis W. Webb, Jr., on June 7, 1961. Courtesy of University Archives

Sidney Oman, mayor of Chesapeake, addressed the cadets and other municipal dignitaries at the campus police academy, a university program which helped to train cadets for service in Hampton Roads police departments. Courtesy of University Archives

Kathe Traynor, left, was just getting started but Jim Welby, below, had been at it for quite a while as these photos from the early 1970s show. Courtesy of University Archives

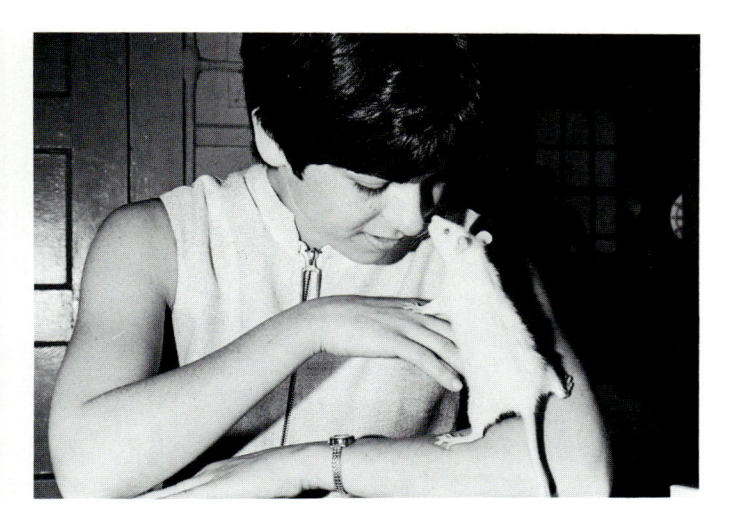

Sometimes student research in the behavioral and natural sciences involves use of animals. In this 1970 picture, an unidentified psychology student saw eye to eye with the subject of her experiment. Courtesy of University Archives; photograph by William Riedell

Throughout its history, the university has had many parents and their children attending classes together at the same time. They have also helped each other working toward degrees. In these two photos from the early 1960s, a mother-daughter and father-son team reflect that strong family effort. Above, Vera Richardson showed the portrait of her daughter Margaret which she painted in Charles Sibley's evening art class. On the right, John Young, Jr., and John Young, Sr., studied together for upcoming exams. Below, President Alfred B. Rollins, Jr., posed with three graduates from the same family. They are Jerry, Jeffrey, and Dennis Kaiser. Courtesy of University Archives

The Environmental Conservation Organization of Students (ECOS) sought to prevent the use of pollutants and to conserve natural resources. Examples of their many activities were the "Save a Branch" campus campaign to encourage recycling of newsprint and the environmental teach-ins which they conducted during the 1970s. The group was also instrumental in establishing the Dismal Swamp Preserve, a permanent ecological treasure for future generations. Courtesy of University Archives

One of the early doctoral programs at the university was in oceanography. In the picture, a student applies his knowledge of the sciences to the study of the oceans. Courtesy of University Archives

In March, 1968, President Lewis W. Webb, Jr., requested that the Army establish an ROTC program on the campus. That spring, the first officers came to campus. Since then, a Navy ROTC unit has become part of the campus cooperative program with Norfolk State University and Hampton University. The two pictures selected here show part of the physical training program of the AROTC and a commissioning ceremony for the NROTC. Courtesy of Public Information Services

The series of photographs on the next two pages illustrate that hands-on-training has always complemented lecture/discussion courses at the university. Courtesy of Public Information Services

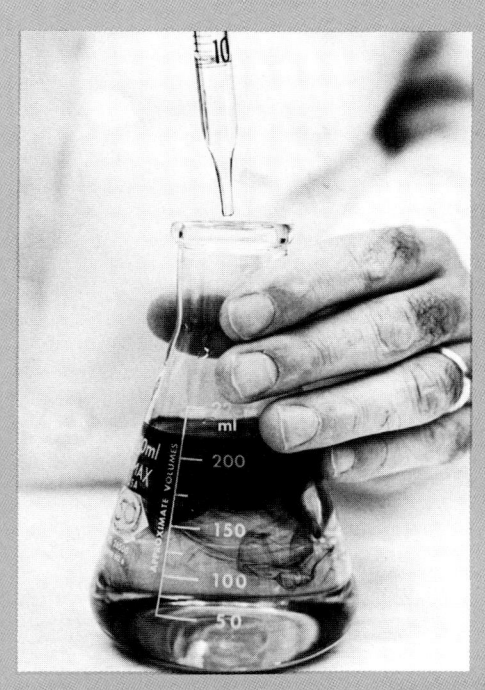

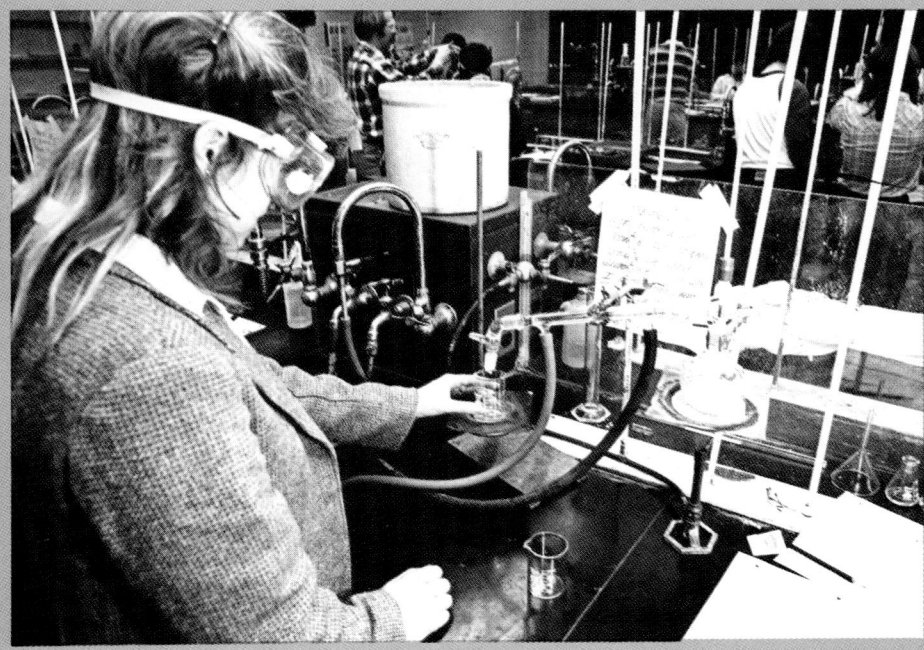

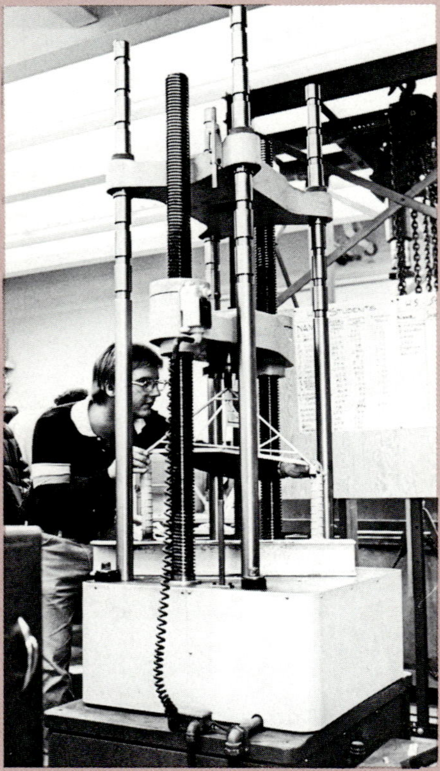

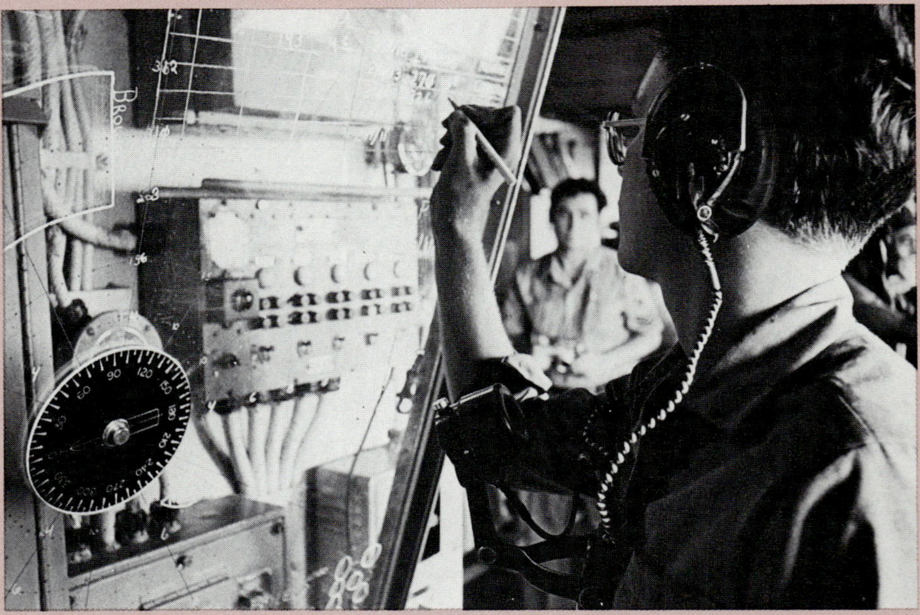

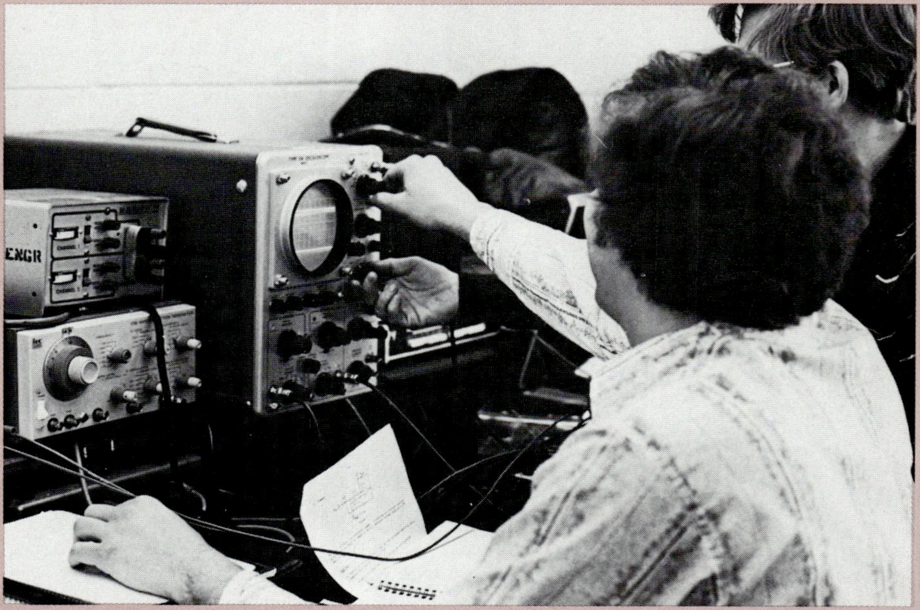
ENGR

The university's mission emphasis on international studies led to student interest in non-Western languages. In the picture, below, Said Abdessamad, a graduate student from Morocco, taught a course in Arabic. On the left, the Japanese Calligraphy Club practiced the art on newspapers. Courtesy of Public Information Services

The Center for Instructional Development makes possible the use of video materials for classroom use, thereby expanding the opportunities for learning through innovative self-paced courses. Courtesy of Public Information Services

Graduation marks the culmination of years of hard work in academe as illustrated in this first formal university August commencement in 1986. Courtesy of Public Information Services

FRATERNITIES AND SORORITIES

The Imps Club, organized on November 5, 1930, was the first men's social organization. By 1932, it had grown from twelve to fifteen, and by 1936, it had thirty members, twenty-seven of whom are shown in the picture. Catherine Cubberly, women's athletics instructor, was the club's sponsor and is shown in the center. The Imps had monthly parties and a dance each semester. School years were capped with a gala banquet and dance each spring. Members were George P. Hand, Jr., president, Robert C. Rawl, vice president, Lewis A. Nuckols, treasurer, and Lucius P. Daugherty, secretary. Others were John R. Ball, W. Meredith Bayne, Jack T. Branch, Jr., I. Lee Chapman, William C. Cotten, Edward Causey Davis, C. Fred Edmonds, M. M. Gregory, Jr., Donald G. Griffin, John Hodges, Edgar Earl Jackson, Robert B. Masengill, James A. Rives, Jr., John Earl Roberts, William Rosenfeld, Donald Smith, George A. Stewart, Jr., Robert W. Stewart, Jr., James A. Swaney, W. R. L. Taylor, Jr., William Weaver, William C. West, and William P. Wise. Courtesy of University Archives

During the 1950s, The Imps and Gamma Gamma sorority had an annual Sadie Hawkins dance. In the picture on the right, Sylvester Brown, left, and Harry Ramsey pretended to capture Lynette Twiford. Below, Edward Cunningham, second from the left, and Patricia Vincent third from the left, joined friends in costume as cartoon characters to advertise the upcoming dance. Courtesy of University Archives

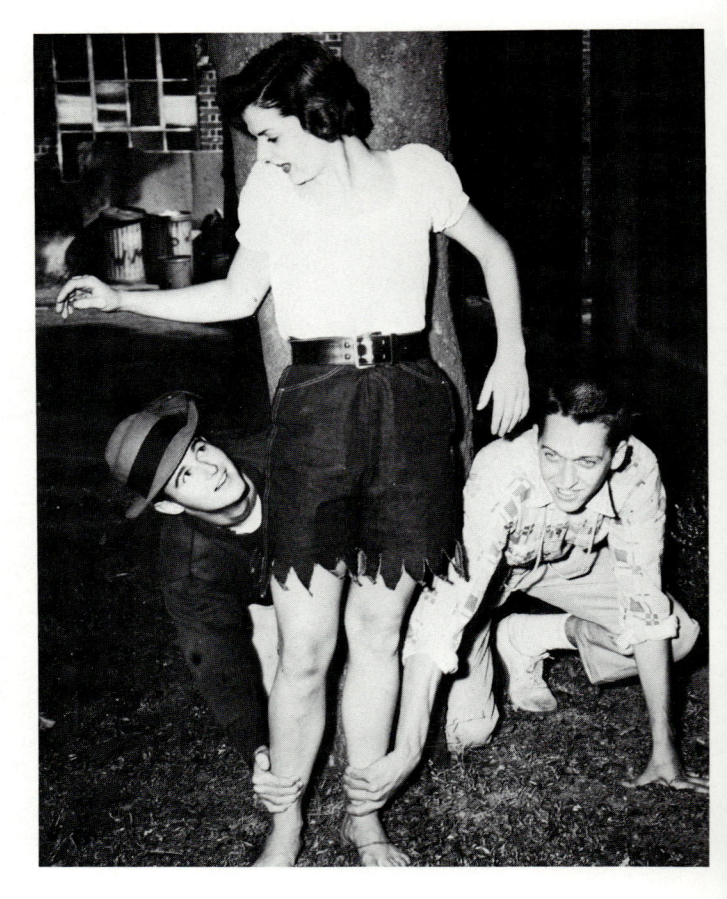

Dorothy Taylor, Bill Ambrose, and Sylvia Miller helped prepare for Pi Phi Sigma fraternity and Gamma Gamma sorority's March Monsoon dance in 1958. Courtesy of University Archives

TIGA fraternity sponsored an informal reception for new graduates in 1956. Gwendolyn Carter congratulated Leigh Stewart on his degree as Mr. and Mrs. Albert B. Gornto, Jr., looked on. Courtesy of University Archives

Attending the 1956 Tri-K sorority's rush party in costume were, left to right, Carol White, Ellen Whitehurst, Jinny Robinson, Betty Renn, Dorothy Mehard, Mary Nolley, and Betty Burns. Courtesy of University Archives

Delta Omega Phi used creative artistry and costuming to advertise the Playboy dance. Courtesy of University Archives

Homecoming King Donald Wirt slipped the magic slipper on the foot of Queen Linda Myers in this photo from the 1950s. Behind the queen were Elbert Bowden, right, and Margaret Davis, second from the right. Courtesy of University Archives

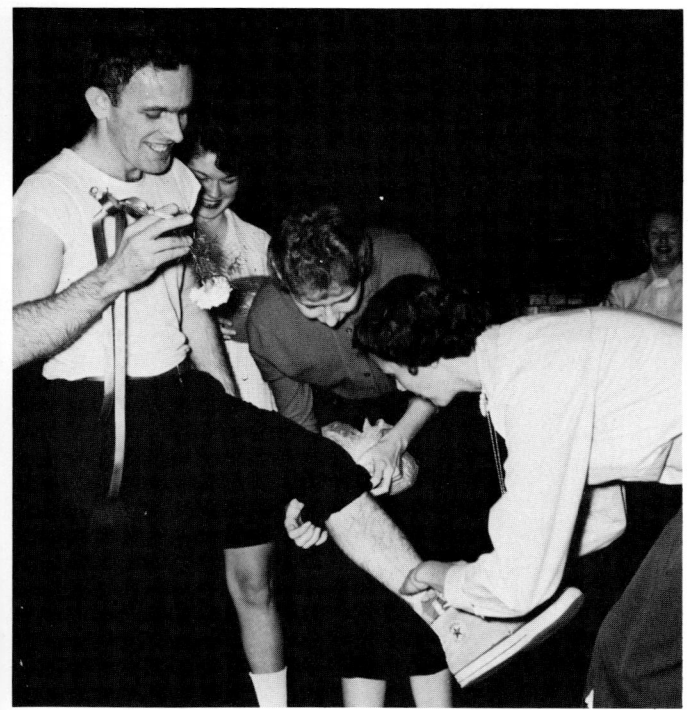

Chosen Tri-K's sweetheart at the basketball game between the Imps fraternity and Tri-K sorority, Arthur Dow of the philosophy department enjoyed the honor of receiving the garter. Courtesy of University Archives

Donna Gilliam, left, Jean Cantley, middle, and Trish Harris of Tri-K sorority geared up for the Hobgoblin Hop in 1961. Courtesy of University Archives

TIGA fraternity sponsored the Bar-T Roundup as an annual dance. To advertise the event in 1961, Kevin Kent was "hanged" by fraternity brothers playing vigilantes. Courtesy of University Archives

101

Greek Week each spring saw events such as the King-of-the-Mountain grease pit and other rollicking antics like those pictured here. From the 1960s, the Volkswagen race and the Imps—Pi Phi Sigma tug-of-war depict some of the fun of a campus tradition. Courtesy of University Archives

The Greek Rock, presented to the university by Theta Xi fraternity, stands on the south side of Kaufman Mall. Courtesy of University Archives

For a small fee, students were able to vent their frustrations on an old car at the TKE fraternity smash in the early 1970s. Courtesy of University Archives

Pi Kappa Alpha brothers paused for a photo before resuming their crab feast in 1971. Courtesy of University Archives

103

PERFORMANCES/ CULTURAL EVENTS

Madrigal Singers under the direction of S. Eliot Breneiser, right, in 1954 were left to right, first row, Nancy Newsome, Tony Cacalano, John Hart, Jack Dent, and Wilie DeLara. In the second row, left to right, were Billie Bell, Anne Kirwan, Betty Cootes, and Carol Brock. At the right, below, Madrigal Singers served in costume their annual dinner in 1979.

Courtesy of University Archives

Courtesy of Public Information Services

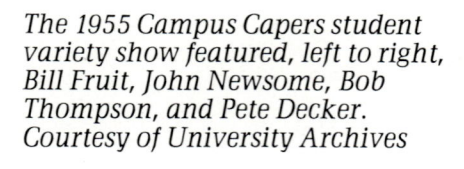

*The 1955 Campus Capers student variety show featured, left to right, Bill Fruit, John Newsome, Bob Thompson, and Pete Decker.
Courtesy of University Archives*

104

The college choir, under the direction of Willard Robb, sang their Christmas program at the Kiwanis Club in 1956. Courtesy of University Archives

Eugene Paxhia directed the band as they rehearsed for the college TV program, "Signposts." Courtesy of University Archives

From left to right, Susan Hodges, Carol Culpepper, and Faith Holmes participated in the Aqua Fantasia Show at the college swimming pool in 1959. Courtesy of University Archives

The university's strong commitment to the visual and performing arts has enriched the lives of everyone in the community. Through plays, ballet, art shows, opera workshops, and musical programs of all kinds, the university through the School of Arts and Letters has been one of the major cultural centers of the Tidewater area. Courtesy of Public Information Services

Over thirty thousand fans packed Foreman Field for the Crosby, Stills, Nash, and Young concert on August 17, 1974. Courtesy of University Archives

A very popular music celebrity and organizer of the annual folk festival on campus during the 1960s and 1970s, Bob Zentz, left, prepared for the sixth festival with Irish singer Jerry Kelley in this picture. Courtesy of Public Information Services

Courtesy of University Archives

Through the years, the university has produced outstanding drama, comedy, and musicals. These scenes from recent Paul Dicklin productions at the Riverview Theater are Dracula, *above*, George M, *right*, and Deathtrap, *bottom*.

Courtesy of Public Information Services

Courtesy of Public Information Services; photograph by Bill Laux

108

CULTURAL ENRICHMENT

During the 1950s and 1960s, the Old Dominion College Concert Series was an outstanding contribution to the cultural life of the students and community-at-large. Held in the Center Theater in downtown Norfolk, these events brought internationally known artists to Tidewater. Van Cliburn, Roberta Peters, and Victoria de los Angeles, pictured here, were three of those artists. Photographs courtesy of University Archives

Tom and Dick Smothers, and Peter, Paul, and Mary illustrate some of the popular performers whom the university brought to the area in the 1960s. Courtesy of University Archives

In the 1970s, university convocation speakers like Benjamin Hooks, Jesse Owens, John Glenn, and Ralph Nader (pictured on the next page) broadened student horizons. Courtesy of University Archives

Caught with his hand in the cookie jar, John Dean nonetheless provided the campus and community a first-hand account of the Watergate scandal. Courtesy of Public Information Services

Maya Angelou was one of many writers who participated in the successful annual Literary Festival. Courtesy of University Archives

SPECIAL EVENTS

The Artie Shaw band provided the jitterbug beat for sailors and students at this September, 1941 dance at Foreman Field. Courtesy of Carroll Walker

This Oyster Bowl Parade float of the mid-1950s depicted activities of campus life. The William and Mary-VPI sweatshirt and the William and Mary sweaters worn by the girls are reminders of the past affiliations of the university. Courtesy of Public Information Services

The college's silver anniversary celebration in 1955 included the selection by Jackie Gleason, nationally known comedian, of a queen for the weekend festivities. Queen Betty Starr Cootes, second from the right in the front row, shared the limelight with her maid of honor Penny Johnston, far right front row. Judy Fowlkes, Jo Ann Virgili, front row left to right, and Billie Bell, Louise Disosway, Patti Thompson, and Carolyn Pillsbury, second row left to right, applauded Gleason's selection. Courtesy of University Archives

Queen Betty Starr Cootes posed in her beautiful gown for the silver anniversary celebration in 1955. Courtesy of University Archives

A small student body in the 1950s and 1960s made the regular student-faculty basketball game an event for the whole college. Following the game, a sock-hop in the gym of the old Administration Building gave spectators and participants alike the opportunity to get to know each other. Courtesy of University Archives

Tri-K sorority's Donna Gilliam and Elizabeth Hechtkopf hoofed their rendition of "Little Men" in the junior class variety show of 1961. Courtesy of University Archives

This student competed in the "Miss Amazon" contest at the junior class carnival in 1964 by donning a grass skirt and doing the hoola. Courtesy of University Archives

"Nursing through the Ages" was the pageant presented by the 1969 health care class. In the first row were, left to right, Lynda Young, Katherine Myatt, Bernice Powles, Nancy Tummons, Jane Hansen, Marie Foltz, Gar Yip, and Margaret Wilson. In the second row, left to right, were Patricia Rapp, Suzanne White, Flora Morgan, Elizabeth Werber, Susan Hurst, Melodie Lambert, Catherine Bacha, Janet Belch, and Earle Ammerman. Courtesy of University Archives

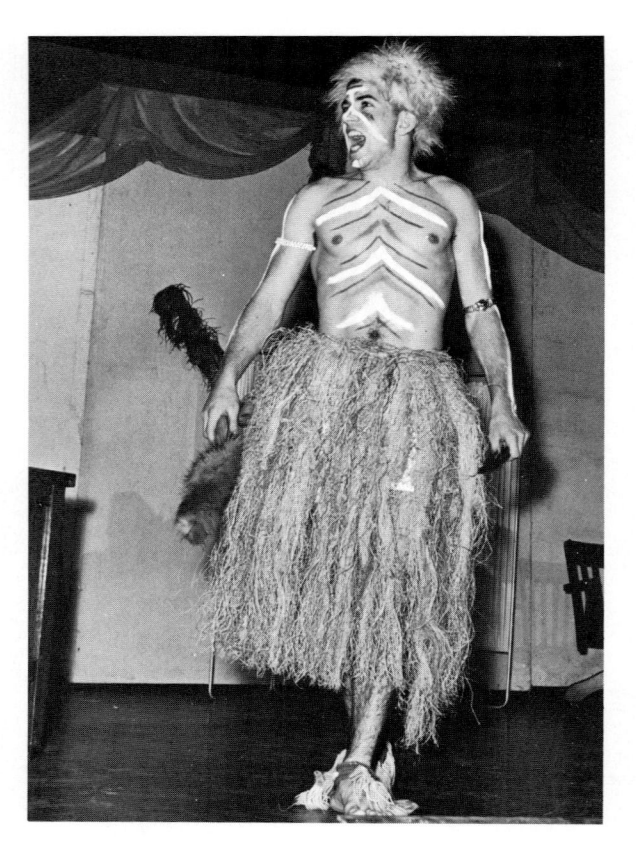

Homecoming dances during the 1960s and 1970s marked the high point of what the Mace and Crown *called "the social event of the school year." At the 1970 Homecoming festivities, Judy Babine was crowned queen. Courtesy of University Archives*

The 1971 Homecoming Court were, left to right, Linda Ribaudo, Lorry Newell, Mae Francis Felton, Queen Gloria Henley, and Lynn Andrews. Courtesy of University Archives

Bill Williams, station engineer, Dick Gaya, station manager and music director, and Conrad Wilson, Jr., member of the English department and faculty adviser, prepared for a program on WMTI-FM, the college radio station, in 1961. At the right, Rusty Carter, a history major, worked as a disc jockey at WODU, the university radio station begun in the early 1970s in Rogers Hall. WODU started with two small transmitters and was a joint student-faculty effort. In the early 1980s, it moved to Webb Center where it grew to a much larger operation. Students were given opportunities not only in broadcast journalism but also in selling ads for the station. Engineering majors assisted with the station. Quite a few of the students who worked there over the years were later employed by local televison and radio stations. Courtesy of University Archives

In fall, 1974, Nicholas J. DeRose, ('76) and some of his friends were looking at the Guiness Book of World Records. *They became convinced that they could set a bed pushing record by wheeling a bed from the university to Washington, D.C. Dean of Students Dana Burnett convinced them to start a muscular dystrophy marathon dance once they discovered that municipalities would not allow them to push a bed to the nation's capital. Thus began the annual Superdance for Muscular Dystrophy, the eighth of which is pictured here. The dance has raised well over $160,000 to aid in the fight against the disease. Courtesy of Public Information Services; photograph by Michael Blanton*

The university sponsored many events "open to the public" as part of its service to the community of Hampton Roads. A large crowd gathered in the Batten Arts and Letters auditorium to participate in the debates over the second Strategic Arms Limitation Treaty (SALT II). Courtesy of University Archives

Neighbors of the university in Lamberts Point enjoyed the annual Christmas party sponsored by university students, faculty, and staff. Courtesy of Public Information Services

The International Jubilee brings people from all over the world to show their native costumes and sell native foods and perform native dances. In this 1986 photo, Spanish dancers received the appreciation of the crowd. Courtesy of Public Information Services

No Homecoming celebration would be complete without a bonfire. This is the university's 1986 effort. Courtesy of Public Information Services

121

PROTESTS OF THE SIXTIES AND SEVENTIES

Armistead L. Boothe, Democratic primary candidate for the United States Senate, found considerable concern among students about American participation in the Vietnam War when he spoke on campus on May 11, 1966. Courtesy of University Archives; photograph by S. H. Ringo

The student-operated Free University offered non-credit courses of interest which people might not be able to get in their regular program of study. These included such topics as "Aspects of the Psychedelic Experience," "Vagabonding Around the World," "The New Left Defined," as well as more traditional themes such as "Contemporary Moral and Social Questions." Courtesy of University Archives

Although the university witnessed considerably less student protest during the late 1960s and early 1970s than did many other campuses across the nation, students did express their opposition to aspects of the war in Vietnam. Others were equally unhappy with the anti-war demonstrators. Dale Kuehn in the upper left voiced the opinion of the Young Americans for Freedom. Photograph by James Turner. Below, a young man protested the bombing of Southeast Asia in 1970. Courtesy of University Archives

Joseph Mimarik, national secretary-treasurer of Americans for Democratic Action, addressed students in front of Webb Center. Below, students condemned arrests made in Washington during May Day demonstrations in 1971. Courtesy of University Archives; photograph by John Paradise

In order to protest what many students considered poorly maintained parking lots and administration unresponsiveness to student senate resolutions of complaint, the students parked in faculty and staff lots for one week. Gordon McDougall, student body president, led a rally at which parking tickets were publicly burned. Later the tickets were appealed, students were found guilty, and fines were suspended.

Gordon is now director of the Alumni Association and secretary to the Board of Visitors. Courtesy of Public Information Services

STUDENT LEADERS

High Hat *staff members preparing one of the 1956 issues of the college newspaper were, left to right, Mary Clay Nichols, Carolee Anderson, Ronald Pierce, M. L. Sallinger, Ken Brown, Neal Alloway, Bill Becker, and Sally Futrell. Courtesy of University Archives*

A mock election on campus in November, 1956, led supporters of the Democrats to bring their mascot to campus. John Newman, Jeannie Cornell, Dick Sullivan, Harry May, and Dot Roberts supported Adlai Stevenson. The Republican elephant who "liked Ike" was also present for the election. Courtesy of University Archives

The Senior Honorary Leadership fraternity was formed in 1959 to recognize scholastic achievement and leadership. Members, front row, left to right, were Harry May, Dorothy Taylor, Ida Faye McMath, Betty Wheeler and Harold McGee. In the back row, left to right, were Richard Rutyna, Jim Dalonas, and Anthony Long. Courtesy of University Archives

The first Young Republican Organization meeting was held on May 6, 1960. Roger Coleman, left, was first chairman of "Youth for Nixon." Betty Lou Parker was district representative and corresponding secretary, and John Dalton, right, was visiting the campus as chairman of the Young Republican Federation of Virginia. Dalton later served as governor of Virginia. Courtesy of University Archives

Senior class President Ron Horne addressed a rally in front of Webb Center in 1969. Standing to his left was Gene Woolard, student body president. Courtesy of University Archives; photograph by Stan Rudacil

John Sasser was student body president during the "Save ODU" campaign in 1970-1971. Courtesy of University Archives

Student body President Rickey Adams met weekly with Dean of Student Affairs Dana Burnett during Adams' term in 1974-1975. Courtesy of Public Information Services

Student body President Keith Curtis and Vice President Jane Ferrara were leaders in the early 1980s. Jane is currently actively working in the Alumni Association helping to establish new chapters around the state. Courtesy of Public Information Services

Being editor of the student newspaper can be a messy job as Mike Gooding illustrated in this 1982 picture. Many of the students who have edited the Mace and Crown have gone on to work for local newspapers and TV stations. Courtesy of Public Information Services

CAMPUS LIFE

The old "Bud's" bookshop and snack bar, shown here about 1955, was a popular gathering place for students. Until 1956, it was in the old Administration Building. It then moved to the back of the Science Building. Courtesy of University Archives

Courtesy of University Archives

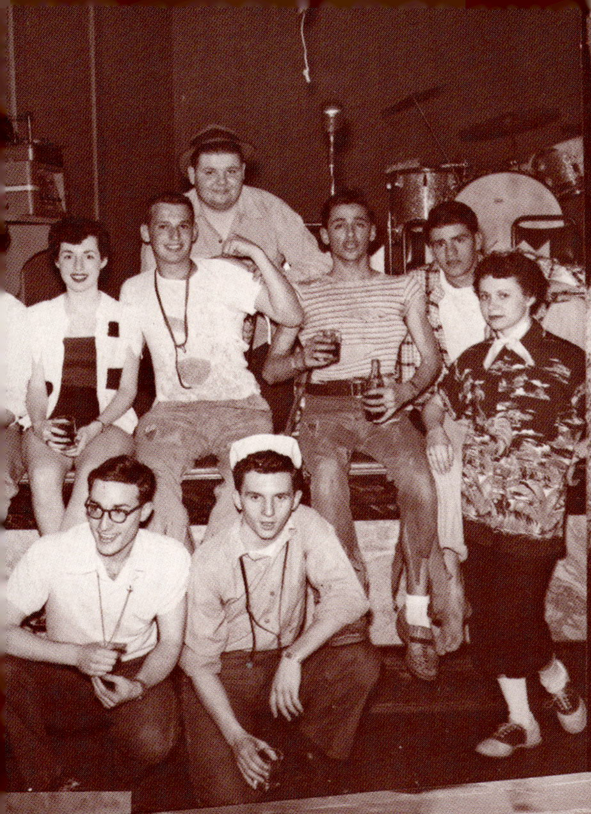

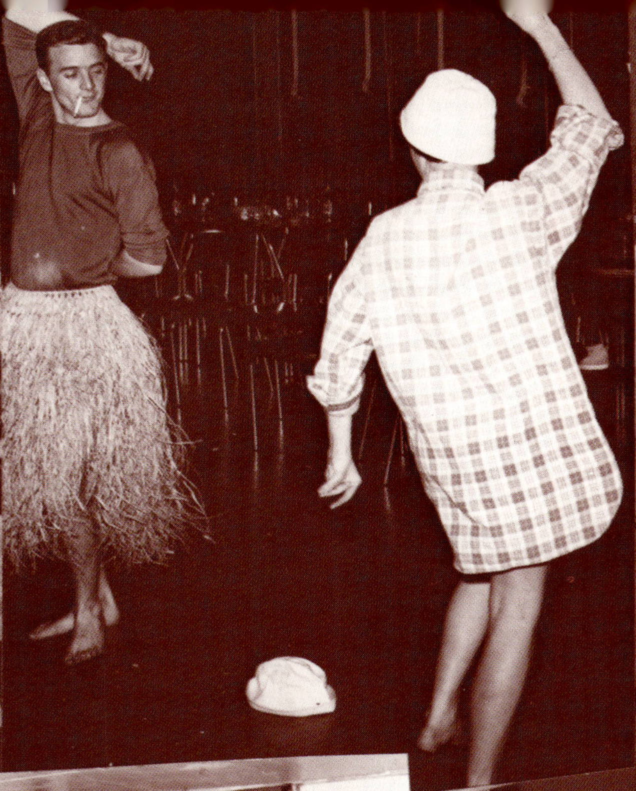

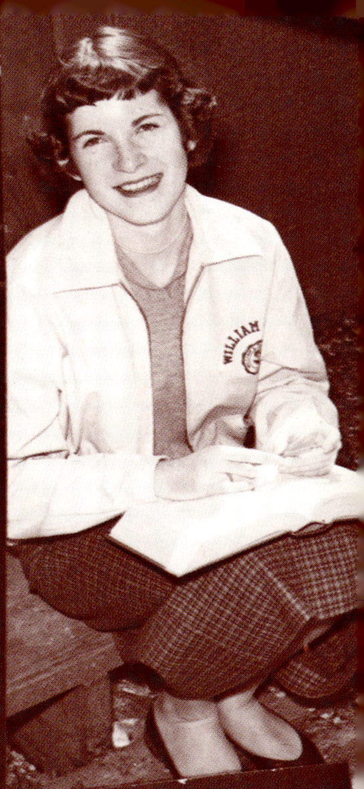
WILLIAM

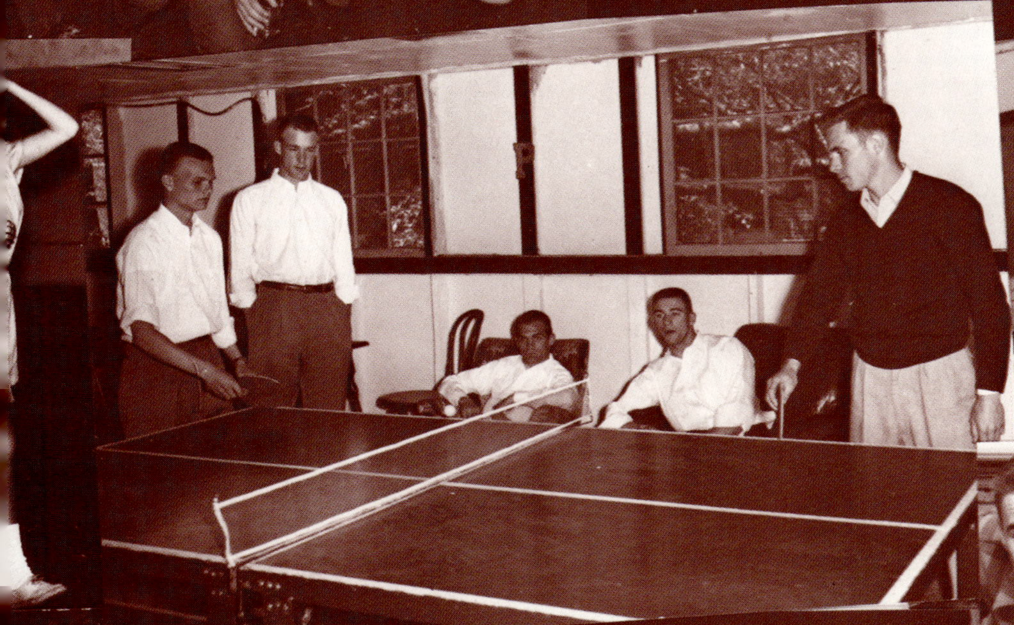

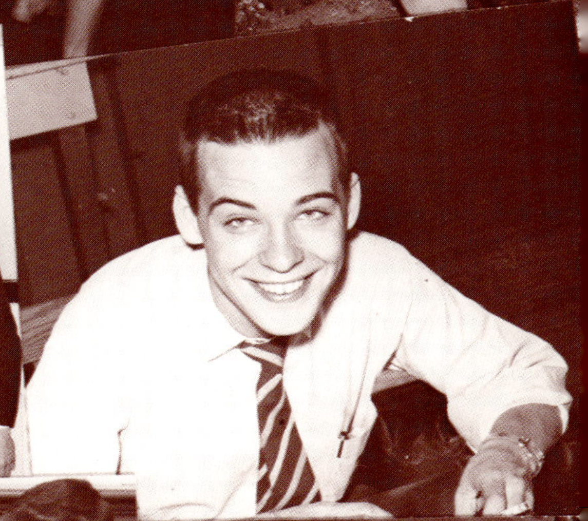

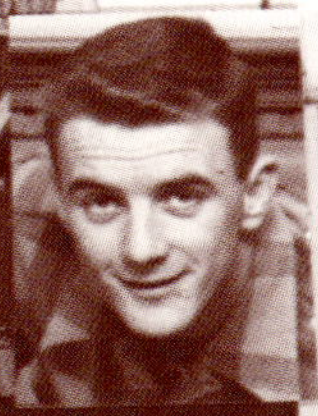

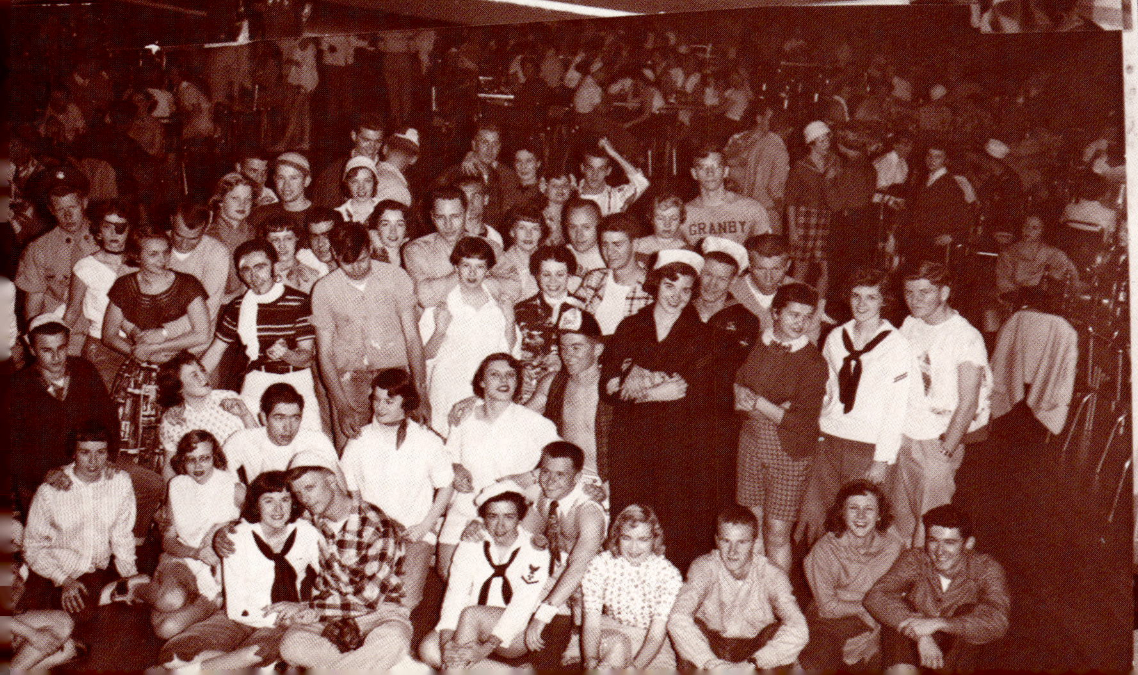
GRANBY

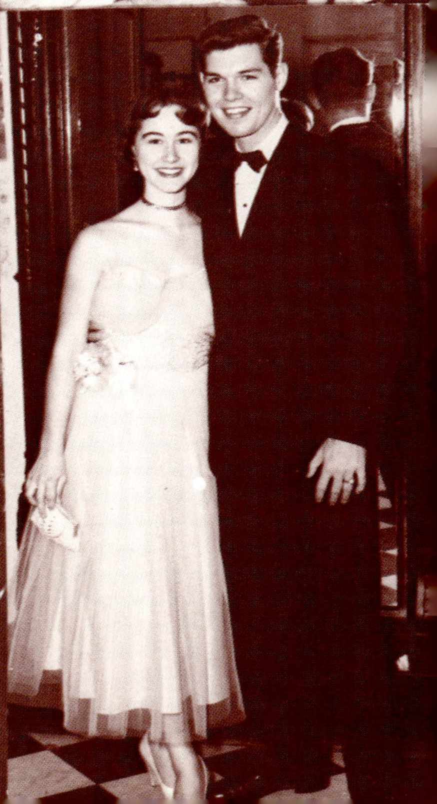

Parking problems at the university are nothing new as these pictures from the 1960s reveal. Courtesy of University Archives; upper photograph by Clifton Guthrie, lower photograph by Peter Harahan

Students worked very hard to get more funding from the legislature in the 1970–1971 "Save ODU" campaign. Courtesy of University Archives; photograph by William Riedell

Letting off steam and apparently enjoying every minute of it, students watered one another down in a dorm raid free-for-all. Courtesy of University Archives

There was not much "streaking" on the campus during the mid-1970s, but the few incidents that occurred caused quite a stir. This picture was taken in 1974. Courtesy of University Archives

Each year the university community honors the memory of the Rev. Martin Luther King, Jr. In the picture at the left, Newport News Mayor Jessie M. Rattley addressed students and faculty at one observance. Below, students marched to honor the non-violent struggle for human rights and dignity for which King lived. Courtesy of Public Information Services

Many student activities take place on Kaufman Mall near Webb Center. The A. Rufus Tonelson Garden provides a place for students to study and for university receptions. The paved area in front provides a gathering place for students during activity hours except on those rare occasions when snow is falling. Courtesy of University Archives

Courtesy of University Archives

Courtesy of Public Information Services

Eight religious denominations have active campus ministries at the university, and the religious community jointly sponsors activities with many faiths. Shown in this photo is a mural in the Baptist Student Center which depicted the faces of young people. Courtesy of Public Information Services

Assisted by students and staff members, Norval Stanaway, assistant director of dining services, center, assembled the gigantic cake commemorating the university's fiftieth birthday in 1980. Courtesy of Public Information Services

Engineering student Tom Wolfgang used his creative art skills to remodel his Powhatan I apartment. The bookshelf, windows, and fireplace are paintings. Courtesy of Public Information Services

In this spring picture, a student enjoyed the warmth of April by hanging out the window for a brief catnap as Garfield contemplated warmer days to come. Courtesy of Public Information Services; photograph by Robert Firek

Rogers Hall dormitory residents and friends took a break from their studies to watch an exciting TV series. Courtesy of University Archives; photograph by James F. Lawrence

Parents and students alike shared the challenges and strains of getting moved into the dormitory. Courtesy of University Archives; photograph by William F. Riedell

The Rathskeller, which is located in Webb Center, provides modern students with a place to meet friends, relax, and enjoy the occasional live entertainment which is provided. Courtesy of Public Information Services

In a typical scene of outdoor activities on campus, John Trembley glided over the tennis courts on his skateboard. Courtesy of Public Information Services

Rap sessions in the dorm are an integral part of the life of every resident. Lasting friendships are often formed as students discuss everything from course assignments to the probability of extraterrestrial visitors. Courtesy of Public Information Services

Residents of Gresham's international floor, Iranian Shahin Sadigh, Korean Hakson Kim, and American William Bivens represented an increasing ethnic pluralism at the university. One of the few state institutions of higher learning to exceed its affirmative action goals, the university is proud of the richness which the diversity of student, faculty, and staff backgrounds brings to the community. Courtesy of Public Information Services

Each year Scots and those who study them gather from the United States, Canada, and Europe for a festival and conference at the university. Here Dorothy Douglas, a 1983 graduate, performed on the bagpipes. Courtesy of Public Information Services

Jim Jarrett became director of athletics at Old Dominion University in 1970. During his sixteen-year tenure in that position, Jarrett has successfully moved the university's athletic program from Division II into Division I competition. Stressing "selective excellence" in the university's programs, Jarrett has been praised widely for his commitment to elevating the status of women's athletics at the university. It is no accident that under his direction, women's teams have captured national championships in three different sports—sailing, basketball, and field hockey. Courtesy of Sports Information Office

Chapter 6

Athletics

For some time after the Norfolk Division was established in 1930, its athletic schedule was filled primarily with local high school, college freshman, and military service teams. By the late 1930s a number of small North Carolina college teams also appeared on the schedule, with an occasional major college team making the schedule in some sports by the 1940s. The decades of the 1930s and 1940s were lean years made even leaner by the Great Depression and World War II. There were not a lot of funds available for such "frills" as college athletics, much less team travel. After the war, the situation began to improve. In the 1950s sports competition gradually came to assume a more important role in college life, at least for men, and that period found the Norfolk Division competing in the "mythical" Little Eight Conference which was composed of Virginia colleges. In 1962, the college joined the Mason-Dixon Conference, continuing to compete in Division II athletics until 1976, at which time the university moved into Division I and joined the southern division of the Eastern College Athletic Conference. The Monarchs joined the Sun Belt Conference in 1982.

Old Dominion University athletes won their first national championship in 1975, in men's Division II basketball. Since moving into Division I in 1976–1977, seven more national championships have been captured by Old Dominion University teams: three in women's basketball (1979, 1980, 1985), three in women's field hockey (1982, 1983, 1984), and one in women's sailing (1982). In addition, university teams have also finished as runners-up in national championship competition on two occasions since 1976: in women's basketball, and in women's field hockey. Old Dominion teams have also won numerous state, Little Eight, Mason-Dixon, Eastern College Athletic Conference, NCAA and Sun Belt regional or divisional championships in a variety of sports.

In the 1985-1986 season, Old Dominion's sixteen intercollegiate teams won more than sixty-five percent of their contests, thus giving them the winningest percentage among all ten Virginia Division I schools for the fourth consecutive year and the seventh time in the past eight years. As of the 1986-1987 season, the men's basketball team had advanced to post-season play in fifteen of the past sixteen years. The women's team had done likewise in nine of the past ten years. In addition, soccer, wrestling, baseball, sailing, and field hockey teams have all broken into the national top twenty ranks.

One of the statistics of which Old Dominion University is proudest, however, is the fact that its student-athletes graduate at a rate well above the national average. Since 1980, Old Dominion has graduated ninety-four percent of its athletes, compared to the national average of fifty percent.

WOMEN'S BASKETBALL

Women's basketball at Old Dominion University has come a long way since the days when some very good teams sponsored by Snow White Cleaners competed in AAU competition with distinction. In more recent times, the Lady Monarchs have established themselves as a formidable national power to be reckoned with. Since 1975, Old Dominion University women athletes have won three national basketball championships. In the 1977-1978 season, the Lady Monarchs won the National Women's Invitational Tournament championship, climaxing a 30-4 season with a tournament victory over the University of Texas. In the 1978-1979 and 1979-1980 seasons, while compiling an unbelievable 72-2 record, the ladies captured two consecutive Association of Intercollegiate Athletics for Women championships, with victories over Louisiana Tech and Tennessee, respectively. In 1984-1985, the Lady Monarchs won their first NCAA national basketball championship and their third national title, with a victory over the University of Georgia. The Lady Monarchs have also won numerous state and regional titles and Sun Belt Conference titles, and for a decade were consistently ranked in the top ten women's basketball teams in the nation.

By 1931, the Norfolk Division had a women's basketball team. They played their first game in March, 1931 against William and Mary's freshman team. Pictured here are the members of the 1934 women's team. Standing, from left to right, were Catherine Cubberly Beamon, the coach, Elizabeth Sanders, manager, Frances Maddrey Healey, an unidentified player, Sally Leigh, Elsie Quinlan, and Anne Whitehurst White. Kneeling, from left to right, were Lucy Arnold, Catherine Moore Gowing, Mildred Cornick, Betsy Wilson Downey, and Mildred Mann Ames. Other women's sports of the 1930s included fencing, swimming, tennis, field hockey, and archery, among others. Courtesy of University Archives

Jean Holloman Whitehurst, shown here shooting over the head of an opponent, was one of the outstanding women's basketball players of the 1950s. Courtesy of Public Information Services

There was cause for celebration following the Lady Monarchs' victory in the 1977-1978 National Women's Invitational Tournament in Amarillo, Texas. But that victory was simply the appetizer before the feast to come, in which the Lady Monarchs would devour the competition and consume three national championships. Courtesy of University Archives

The Lady Monarchs' 1978-1979 AIAW national championship team is shown in this photograph. Kneeling, from left to right, were Sue Brown, Sandy Burke, Debbie Richard, Sue Davy, Beth Campbell, and Fran Clemente. Standing, from left to right, were Coach Marianne Stanley, Nancy Lieberman, Jan Trombly, Sue Richardson, Inge Nissen, Linda Jerome, Chris Critelli, Rhonda Rompola, Angela Cotman, and Assistant Coach Jerry Busone. Courtesy of Sports Information Office

In 1985 the Lady Monarchs won the NCAA Division I National Championship in women's basketball. In recognition of that accomplishment, they were invited to the White House to receive the congratulations of President Ronald Reagan. Shown here, with the President, were the members of that championship team and other university representatives. Standing from left to right, they were Alfred B. Rollins, Jr., president of the university, Marie Christian, Adrienne Goodson, Donna Harrington, Lisa Blais, Tracy Claxton, Coach Marianne Stanley with the championship game ball, Medina Dixon, Dawn Cullen, Liz Connahan, Alphelia Jenkins, Bridget Jenkins, and Robert M. Stanton, rector of the Board of Visitors. Courtesy of the White House

146

Four great women's basketball players are featured in this series of photographs.

Inge Nissen, an All-American in 1978 and 1979. Courtesy of Sports Information Office

Medina Dixon, an All-American in 1985. Courtesy of Sports Information Office

Nancy Lieberman, a three-time All-American, led the team to two national championships. Courtesy of Sports Information Office

Anne Donovan, an All-American in 1981 and 1982. Courtesy of Sports Information Office

MEN'S BASKETBALL

The men's basketball program traces its origins back to the very first year in the history of the Norfolk Division. Tom Scott coached the basketball team during its first decade. Bud Metheny coached the team from 1948 until 1965, when he was succeeded by Sonny Allen. Allen coached the team for ten years, and was followed as coach by Paul Webb in 1975. Webb relinquished the team to Tom Young in 1985. Throughout this period, as was the case with other sports, the basketball program progressed gradually as early opponents, high school teams and freshman college teams, came to be replaced with stiffer competition. The college advanced to Division III, then to Division II in 1965, and finally in 1976 to Division I status. Along the same lines, the college advanced into the Little Eight Conference, then into the Mason-Dixon Conference in 1962. Old Dominion then competed in the Eastern College Athletic Conference before joining the Sun Belt Conference. Since 1958, eighteen Old Dominion basketball players have received All-American honors. Twelve players have been professionally drafted. Five players have had their jerseys retired—Wilson Washington, Joel Copeland, Dave Twardzik, Leo Anthony, and Mark West.

Pictured here are the members of the 1930-1931 Norfolk Division basketball team. In the front row, from left to right, were A. Rufus Tonelson, Alex Segal, Harry Hamburger, Sidney Sacks, and Sam Phillips. In the second row, from left to right, were Dave Nesson, Foy Vann, Truman Baxter, and John Rydeen. In the third row, left to right, were Coach Tommy Scott, H. Edgar Timmerman, the director of the Norfolk Division, and Harry Taylor. The team's first game and victory was against South Norfolk High School. Courtesy of University Archives

The 1975 NCAA Division II national champion Old Dominion University Monarchs were, from left to right, in the first row, Gray Eubank, Joey Caruthers, Windell Morrison, Dave Moyer, Oliver Purnell, Leon Hylton, Jeff Fuhrmann, Joey O'Brien, and Curtis Cole. In the second row, were Mike Wrigley, Carol Hudson, Jr., Rich Tackaberry, Tommy Street, Jay Rountree, Wilson Washington, Sonny Allen, Charlie Woollum and Ed Hall. The team finished the season with a 25-6 record as well as the national championship. Courtesy of Sports Information Office

One indication of how far men's basketball has come is to be found in the site at which home games are played. In the early days, games were played in the "old gym" which was located in the Administration Building. That facility is pictured in this photograph taken at a game between the Norfolk Division and Hampden-Sydney College in 1960. The balcony seats could hold about six hundred fans, and bleacher-seating was also limited. The "home court" was moved to the Norfolk City Arena for a few years before the new field house opened in 1970. Courtesy of University Archives

149

In 1976, the men's home games were completely moved to Norfolk Scope. As can be seen in this photograph, the new site was much larger. The women's team continued to play most of its home games at the field house, though they also played several key contests at Scope over the years. Courtesy of University Archives

Paul Webb coached the "Runnin' Monarchs" of Old Dominion University from 1975 to 1985, at which time he resigned after twenty-nine years as a college coach. Webb closed his career as the winningest coach in Virginia, and one of the winningest coaches in the country, with a 511-257 record. Before coming to Old Dominion as the successor to Sonny Allen, Webb coached for nineteen years at Randolph-Macon College in Ashland, Virginia. At Old Dominion, he compiled a 196-99 record in ten years. Courtesy of Public Information Services

Tom Young succeeded Paul Webb as coach of the "Big-Blue" in August, 1985. He came to the university from Rutgers and was the seventh winningest Division I coach in the nation with a 457-249 record. In his first season at the helm, he directed the Monarchs to a 23-8 season, a regular season Sun Belt Conference championship, and a bid to the NCAA East Regionals. Courtesy of Sports Information Office

There was always a lot of good action at Old Dominion University basketball games. Exciting fast-break basketball was raised to a fine art under the direction of Coach Sonny Allen. Courtesy of University Archives

*Bobby Johnson
Courtesy of University Archives*

*Jeff Krasnow
Courtesy of University Archives*

Ronnie Valentine
Courtesy of University Archives

Mark West
Courtesy of University Archives

Kenny Gattison
Courtesy of University Archives

From time to time, some important people have been known to "impersonate" Old Dominion University Monarchs, as was the case when author and lecturer George Plimpton visited campus for a convocation address. Courtesy of Public Information Services

FOOTBALL

The Norfolk Division had a football team from 1930 to 1941, during which time they won sixty-two games, lost nineteen, and tied four. The first game was played September 26, 1930, against Suffolk High School. Suffolk won, 7–0. According to university historian James R. Sweeney, lack of attendance at the games, the high costs associated with football, and a substantial debt were among the major reasons for the demise of the football program.

This photograph depicts the first edition of the Norfolk Division football team in 1930. Courtesy of University Archives

In 1935, the Norfolk Division defeated Gallaudet College in football. Most of the teams which the college played were high school, service, and college freshman squads, including that of William and Mary. Courtesy of University Archives

153

BASEBALL

The baseball program at the university is built upon a solid foundation that dates back to the 1930-1931 season at the Norfolk Division under coach Tommy Scott. During Bud Metheny's tenure as coach from 1948 to 1980, his teams had winning seasons in twenty-seven out of thirty-two years. Included among those victories were two NCAA Eastern Regional College Division championships, eight Little Eight Conference championships, and four Mason-Dixon Conference championships. Mark Newman succeeded Metheny as coach in 1980 and has subsequently brought his teams to four top twenty national rankings while compiling a 194-76-2 record, including a 1985 season that saw his team win fifty games, the most ever in a season in the university's history. Under Newman, the team has twice finished as runner-up in the ECAC Tournament, has twice played in the NCAA East Regionals, has won a Sun Belt East Division championship, and in 1985 won the Sun Belt Conference championship. To Newman, "excellence" is the name of the game.

The Norfolk Division baseball team played its first game against Deep Creek High School. The college won behind the pitching of A. Rufus Tonelson. Most of the college's early opponents were members of the Tidewater Scholastic League, or freshman college and junior college teams. This picture of the baseball team was taken during the 1931 season. By 1940, the baseball program at the college had been dropped "because of the expense, lack of suitable opponents, and lack of facilities," according to James R. Sweeney. While no games were played during the 1939-1940 season, the program was soon resurrected and play was resumed during the 1940-1941 season. Pictured here, from left to right in the front row, were Joseph Schnitzer, Al Wilson, Richard Bacchus, A. Rufus Tonelson, and Marion Kelley. In the second row, from left to right, were Dave Nesson, Nathaniel Parks, Fred Stewart, and Philip Stroud. In the third row, from left to right, were Bernard Rosenfeld, the manager, Francis Morrisette, H. Edgar Timmerman, the director of the Norfolk Division, and Coach Tommy Scott. Players not pictured included Terry Maxey, William Abrams, Harry Hamburger, Truman Baxter, and Joseph Berman. Courtesy of University Archives

In both 1963 and 1964, the Monarchs' baseball team won the NCAA College Division Eastern Regional Championship. This picture of the 1964 team was taken in center field at Yankee Stadium in New York, where the championship game was played. Pictured from left to right, in the first row, were: Bill Bigger, Bobby Walton, Fred Balmer, Ray Nelson, Mel Renn, Gene Johnson, Fred Edmonds, Frank Zadell, Fred Kovner, Bill Yeargan, and Wayne Parks. Standing, from left to right, were: Tommy Harrell, Lee McDaniels, John Ward, and Jim Zadell. Courtesy of University Archives

The Bud Metheny Baseball Complex, which was completed in the summer of 1983, is said to be one of the finest collegiate baseball facilities on the East Coast. Courtesy of Sports Information Office

Baseball coach Mark Newman. Courtesy of Sports Information Office

Three baseball All-Americans of the modern era are, from left to right, Todd Azar,...

Wiley Lee...

and, Kevin Bearse. Courtesy of Sports Information Office

WRESTLING

The wrestling program at the university, has been very successful, thanks largely to Coach Pete Robinson. Robinson coached at the university for twenty-six years until his retirement in 1983. A powerhouse in Division II Mason-Dixon Conference competition, the university's wrestling teams have also performed very respectably since the university moved into Division I in 1976-1977. One indication of Robinson's successful coaching can be seen in the fact that under his guidance Old Dominion produced twelve Division II All-Americans and four Division I All-Americans, some of whom have joined him as members of the Old Dominion University Sports Hall of Fame.

With wrestlers, it is sometimes hard to tell which end is up. In this 1961 photograph, Ronnie Davis of Old Dominion was standing his American University opponent on his head. Courtesy of University Archives

158

One of the greatest wrestlers in the university's history was Division I All-American Buddy Lee, Jr., who owns seventeen school records. Lee's 1978-1979 statistics included a 40-1-1 season record. He was a four-time eastern regional champion, and a two-time All-American. Courtesy of Sports Information Office

In this 1970 wrestling scene, the competitors seem to be in the process of creating a new hold to be known henceforth as the "pretzel" hold. Courtesy of University Archives

TRACK and FIELD

Old Dominion University men's track and field flourished during the days of the Norfolk Division and well into the late 1960s, but it has languished since that time. In the early years, the Norfolk Division fielded some very formidable teams which starred such greats as John Brown, a member of the Old Dominion University Sports Hall of Fame. Under the guidance of "Scrap" Chandler and later Lou Plummer, both of whom are also Sports Hall of Fame members, teams from the college participated very successfully in the "mythical" Little Eight Conference and subsequently in the Mason-Dixon Conference. Men's and women's track was reinstated in 1980 but discontinued in 1984. Cross country track made a comeback in the 1980s with the team competing in the Sun Belt Conference.

This photograph of the track team from the 1939-1940 season features what was undoubtedly the strongest team fielded by the Norfolk Division in the early decades of the college's history. From left to right, those pictured in the first row were, Roy Sutton, Cecil Griffin, John Brown, Gil Lawson, and Gus Karnezis. In the second row were Dorsey Cooper, Bodie Wiggins, an unidentified athlete, Cecil Blackwell, and John Borum. In the third row were Coach Tommy Scott, an unidentified assistant, John Peterson, Forrest Dryden, Paul Smith, and an unidentified assistant. Courtesy of University Archives

Pictured here are the members of the 1959-1960 cross country track team. From left to right in the first row, were Steele McGonegal, Buddy Meredith, co-captain of the team, Dave Burgess, the other co-captain, Ronnie Davis, and Norris Jones. Standing, from left to right, were Coach Lou Plummer, Larry Crickenberger, Bob Copley, Oliver Todd, Chuck Fields, and Clem Dalton. Courtesy of University Archives

In 1961, Old Dominion University Sports Hall of Fame hurdler Bobby James scored a win in the high hurdles in a meet with Randolph-Macon College. James is at the far right. Seen with him here were Joe McDonough, on the left, and Sam Thomas, in the center. Courtesy of University Archives

Lady Monarch cross country star Denise Krepshaw is shown here running in front of the competition in the annual Old Dominion University Invitational. Courtesy of Sports Information Office

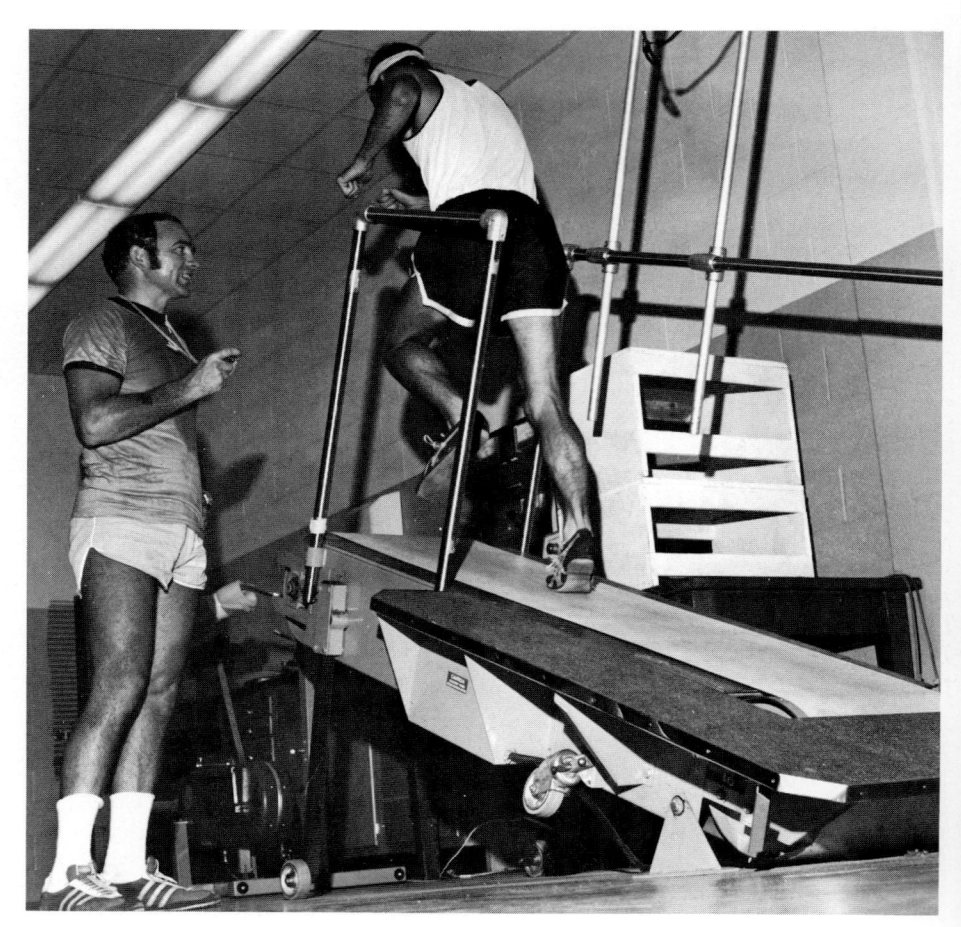

Track coach and running specialist Mel Williams is shown here, on the left, putting one of his 1970s trackmen through some rigorous uphill training. Himself a competitor in distance races, Williams is a noted authority in the field of health medicine. Courtesy of University Archives

WOMEN'S FIELD HOCKEY

The women's field hockey program at the university is founded upon a strong tradition of excellence in that sport which extends back to the early history of the Norfolk Division. The 1956-1957 team pictured here was but one of many teams representing that strong tradition. Shown here, in the front row, from left to right, were Betty Hoggard, Patsy Norman, Carol Jean Kaufman, Mary Ann Hutchinson, and Margaret Hutchinson. In the second row, from left to right, were Coach Emily Pittman, Virginia Miller, Phyllis Mehard, Donna Doyle, Ida Faye McMath, Connie Rowe, Linda Myers, Pat Vincent, and Claudette Whittemore. Courtesy of University Archives

During the years 1982, 1983, and 1984, Old Dominion University women's field hockey teams "gave lessons" on the sport, winning consecutive NCAA national championships in those three years. In 1985, they finished second in the NCAA championships. During the three championship years, the women's field hockey teams compiled an impressive 62-2-0 record. Representing those teams here are the 1983 champions. Pictured from left to right, in the front row, were Dawn Hill, Eveline Veraart, Adele Mears, Christy Morgan, Cindy Wallace, Joyce Cutler, and Jackie Grady. In the second row, from left to right, were head coach and Olympian Beth Anders, Lynn Currie, Ingrid Wold, Cheryl Van Kuren, Stelly Seltmann, Diane Bracalente, Maureen Aikens, Jennifer Walsh, Donna Rodio, Joanne Powers, Carin Peterson, and assistant coaches Char Morett and Marcia Karwas. Courtesy of Sports Information Office

SOCCER

Building on the foundation established by coaches Steve Cottrell, Guenther Dietz, and Bill Killen, since 1970, and the star performances of such earlier soccer greats as Ralf Barner, Mike Valantassis, and Jae Cho, coach Mike Berticelli led the 1985 edition of the soccer team to its winningest season ever. That team posted a record of 16-1-3 and finished second in the Sun Belt Conference Tournament. Shown here were the members of the 1985 team, including from left to right in the first row: Mike Rouette, Randy Winslow, Anthony Beck, Kevin Walsh, Mike Sweeney, Tim Borer, Vincent Beck, Joe Cirrincione, Jan-Olov Aas, David Flores, and Sean Crowley. Standing, from left to right, were: Rob Tymchyshyn, Peter Gaynor, Craig Liberatore, David Dia, Ricardo Daestrella, Simon Toms, Jim Mott, Ken Jewel, Mike O'Neil, Mike Peckwith, Pat Preston, Bill Weyers, and Jon Parker. Courtesy of Sports Information Office

SWIMMING

The university has produced some excellent swimming teams which were very competitive, particularly in the early days of Little Eight, Division II and Mason-Dixon Conference competition. Outstanding individual performances by such swimmers as Mary Fleet Sutton and James W. Clark III in the 1970s have earned them membership in the Old Dominion University Sports Hall of Fame. Pictured here, in a 1961 meet with Randolph-Macon College held in the old pool, were L. Griffin, just to the right of the board, and Duane Beacham, on the right. The swimming team has competed in the modern Olympic-sized pool in the field house since that facility opened in 1970. The new pool is named for former coach Joseph C. "Scrap" Chandler who was the swimming coach from 1942 until 1965. Courtesy of University Archives

TENNIS

The university has produced many fine tennis teams over the years. This team is representative. After winning the Mason-Dixon Southern Division championship, this 1968-1969 team went on to defeat Loyola of Baltimore for the Mason-Dixon Conference championship. Pictured kneeling, from left to right, were Eddie Ettner, Jim Rosemergy, who was captain of the team, Doug Cherry, and Pete Guy. Standing, from left to right, were Coach Al Tatem, Calvin Crafford, Ron Boykin, Bob Lieder, and Marc Balmuth. Women's tennis has a history at the university which extends back to the 1930s. One of the most accomplished competitors in that sport was Pat Shaulis who finished 81–20 overall and qualified for the AIAW regionals every year from 1977–1981. Courtesy of University Archives

SAILING

As the university is located near the Elizabeth River, the Chesapeake Bay, and the Atlantic Ocean, it is only natural that a strong sailing program would develop. Several strong teams have been launched in recent years, but none has been better than the 1982 women's team, which won the National Intercollegiate Yacht Racing Association national sailing championship (the Gerald C. Miller Trophy), which is the equivalent of an NCAA championship. Pictured here is Coach Gary Bodie, who was largely responsible for that championship and the excellent sailing program which it represented. Courtesy of Sports Information Office

LACROSSE

The lacrosse team at the Norfolk Division in the 1940s played some formidable opponents. The 1948 team, pictured here, had on its schedule such teams as the Duke Blue Devils, the Johns Hopkins B-Team, the U.S. Naval Academy Plebes, and Washington and Lee. From left to right, in the first row, the team members were Frank Eng, Marty Rosencrans, William Hickey, C. Hickey, Ralph Murrell, John Romanus, and Corky Tyler. Standing, from left to right, the team members were Edgar A. Kovner, the coach, Jack Lorber, Emmett Jones, Ira Sellers, William Atwood, Robert Stewart, and Curtis Estes. Other lacrosse players of that time, and not pictured, were Emmett Nesbit, D. Brown, Tiny Garrett, George Conwell, Robert West, and Russell Pollard. This picture was taken in May, 1948 at Duke University. In the late 1940s, the Norfolk Division also had men's teams in baseball, basketball, swimming, track, fencing, golf, and weightlifting. Women's lacrosse was begun at the university in 1980, but there has been no men's team in the sport since the 1940s. Courtesy of University Archives

GYMNASTICS

In the early 1970s, the university had a gymnastics team. Pictured here are members of the 1972 team. From left to right, the team members were, Head Coach Gerald George, J. Cookson, R. Blackman, R. Shackleford, C. Davis, J. Tolley, K. Puffenberger, M. Dean, G. Sacks, R. Joy, who was captain of the team, and B. Bourdelaise. Courtesy of University Archives

GOLF

Golf was not organized as a sport at the university until 1959. Thomas M. "Pete" Robinson became coach of the golf team in 1965 and quickly led them to Mason-Dixon Conference championships in 1966 and 1969. Consistent strong play has characterized the efforts of the golf team in the ensuing years. Rich Pruchnik, pictured here, is a player of the modern era who has led the team to a state title and two second place finishes in the Sun Belt Conference. Courtesy of Sports Information Office

THE CHEERLEADERS

The loyalty and enthusiasm which they bring to athletic contests make the cheerleaders important "participants" in those contests. They help to energize the fans on behalf of Monarch teams, and often provide interesting entertainment in demonstrating their own athletic prowess. Shown here in a 1950s photograph as they prepared to raise a "war chant" on behalf of the home team, were, from left to right Sandra LaCasio, Gale Hochban, Loretta Myers, Carol Culpepper, Faith Holmes, and Susan Hodges. Courtesy of University Archives

Marie Hinderliter was a member of the cheerleading squad in the early 1970s. Courtesy of University Archives

Marcia White, also a cheerleader in the early 1970s, here displays some of the wide-ranging emotions experienced by both spectators and cheerleaders during the course of a contest. One minute it is "Darn that old referee..." Courtesy of University Archives

And the next it is "Awwwwww." Courtesy of University Archives

But there are also moments of exultation, as demonstrated in this photograph of 1980s cheerleader Sophia Basil and friend. Courtesy of Sports Information Office

These cheerleaders are "professionals" and recommend that you not try this stunt at home. Courtesy of University Archives

INTRAMURALS

Intramural contests waged between social fraternities or dormitories are an important part of student life. This football game is representative of that aspect of nonvarsity athletic competition. The identifiable players are, from left to right, Joe Bowab, with the ball, Glenn McGrath, and Denny Kendall. Courtesy of University Archives

Powderpuff football is not very typical perhaps, but it is very interesting. In this contest which pitted Pi Beta Phi against Chi Omega, Joan Barry, with the ball, seems to be heading for big trouble as Linda Day and True Lublin close in on her. Courtesy of University Archives

174

OLD DOMINION UNIVERSITY
Sports Hall of Fame

The Old Dominion University Sports Hall of Fame was established in 1980 to honor former athletes, coaches, and administrators who have distinguished themselves and the university by their performance. It is an illustrious group of men and women. The story of their individual achievements serves well to highlight some of the most important moments and developments in the history of athletics at Old Dominion University.

THOMAS L. SCOTT

Tommy Scott, who coached four sports and also served as athletic director during the first eleven years after the Norfolk Division of the College of William and Mary was founded, established lasting standards for success and sportsmanship. Scott fielded winning teams in football, basketball, baseball, and track from 1930 to 1941, when he retired to a business career. He also taught trigonometry, algebra, and other courses. Scott's 1932 grid squad earned a 9-1 record and the distinction of playing in a post-season game that was billed the following year as the Orange Bowl. Twelve thousand fans saw the University of Miami beat the visiting Braves by a 6-2 score. The won-lost slate for the Braves' first six years shows the football team with a 44-12-2 record, basketball a 95-26, and baseball a 58-22. Tommy Scott's remarkable influence in the formative years of the athletic program is reflected even today in an endowed scholarship and an annual award bearing his name. He died in July 1962.
Courtesy of Sports Information Office

A. RUFUS TONELSON

The first student-athlete to enroll at the Norfolk Division of the College of William and Mary when it opened in 1930, A. Rufus Tonelson could look back on fifty years of active participation in athletic and academic programs when he was inducted into the Sports Hall of Fame in 1980. He lettered in basketball for three years, from 1930 to 1933, and captained the 1932 and 1933 teams. He lettered in baseball for three years, from 1931 to 1933, and despite the nickname "Poopball," had a 15-2 record. He was the leading pitcher in the Tidewater Interscholastic Baseball League in 1932. He assisted Tommy Scott in coaching the Norfolk Division's basketball and baseball teams from 1933 to 1936. After serving another alma mater, Maury High in Norfolk, as coach, teacher, and principal, Tonelson returned to Old Dominion in 1966 as a professor of education. Later, after serving as dean of the School of Education, he was selected to become assistant to the president for school and community relations. He retired in 1976. Tonelson and his wife, Sara, another ardent fan who also attended the university, have established an endowed athletic scholarship fund to benefit men basketball and baseball players and women athletes.
Courtesy of Sports Information Office

JOSEPH C. CHANDLER

Thousands of college and high school athletes compete in track and swimming competitions that Scrap Chandler helped to orginate as long ago as 1924. His renown as an athlete and a coach has earned him a spot in the Virginia Sports Hall of Fame as well as the Old Dominion University Sports Hall of Fame. A small man who captained both baseball and track teams at the College of William and Mary, Chandler hit several tape measure home runs and raced to records in 880 and mile competition. Hired by the Tribe as a coach upon graduation in 1924, he brought them ICAA membership, a track distinction that belongs to no other college south of the Mason-Dixon line. Chandler transferred to the Norfolk Division in 1942 to become coach, athletic director and head of the health and physical education program. He coached baseball and basketball until 1948. He retired as athletic director in 1963 and gave up swimming in 1965 but continued as co-coach of the track team until he retired in 1969. A fully endowed athletic scholarship commemorates his many contributions and enables other outstanding athletes to carry on in his tradition. The Old Dominion swimming pool also has been named in his honor, partly in recognition of nearly thirty thousand Virginia youngsters who have learned to swim in a program he established in the mid-1940s. *Courtesy of Sports Information Office*

DONNA DOYLE SMITH

Donna Doyle Smith was a leader on and off the playing fields and courts. A star in basketball, field hockey and tennis, and a dean's list student, she became the namesake for the first athletic scholarship for women at Old Dominion University in 1975. The Donna Doyle Athletic Scholarship Fund gives assistance to female athletes in all women's sports at the university. Named the most outstanding female athlete at the Norfolk Division in 1955, she became the school's first woman physical education graduate in 1958. Her exploits in basketball and golf were notable. She averaged thirty points for ten years while playing with the "Snow White" AAU women's team of Norfolk in state and national competition. A scratch golfer, she turned down an offer from a sporting goods firm to sponsor her on the professional golfing circuit, preferring to pursue a teaching career. She led the "Snow-White" teams to three national tournaments and was named to the all-star team of the World Tournament of the Women's Basketball Association in 1962. She earned berths on the all-star team of the state AAU tournament 1954-1960 and was most valuable player in the 1954 tournament. Donna was the Virginia women's AAU free throw champion in 1953 and 1954. *Courtesy of Sports Information Office*

LEO ANTHONY

The first basketball All-American to play for Old Dominion University, Leo Anthony held eleven of Old Dominion's thirteen cage records when he graduated in 1961. The six-foot guard finished his basketball career in February, 1961 by scoring sixty points against Lynchburg College and becoming the third-highest scorer in state history. Besides earning All-American honors, Anthony was named to the All-Virginia team four times and twice was voted as player of the year in Virginia. As the 1979-80 season began, Anthony still held scoring marks for most points (2,181), highest average in a season (31.0), and highest career average (26.6). With Anthony setting the pace the Braves achieved a four-year record of 55-27 against such teams as Lynchburg, Randolph-Macon, Baltimore, Atlantic Christian, and Roanoke. In addition to starring for four years in basketball, Anthony also started at shortstop for four years in baseball. He was a fluid fielder with great range. Anthony began the 1979-80 season as basketball coach at Princess Anne High School in Virginia Beach holding a career record of 226 wins and 91 losses. *Courtesy of Sports Information Office*

JOHN BROWN

Johnny Brown, one of the greatest natural athletes in the South in the early 1940s, was once compared to Jim Thorpe because of his prowess and versatility in track, football, and baseball. He excelled for the Norfolk Division before winning acclaim on a star-studded Army team packed with All-Americans, and then competing for William and Mary. A high-scoring tailback, a leading hitter in baseball, and top scorer on the track team, Brown scored six firsts in one track meet and set a state AAU long jump record of 22′ 11″ in 1940. In 1946, after having been away from track for five years, he won a college pole vault event with one jump with a borrowed pole. The former dean's list student, hired by the Norfolk school system in 1948, coached outstanding Granby High School track and football teams before becoming principal there. Brown also found time to play professional football with the Norfolk Shamrocks, as well as earn all-star honors and batting titles in Norfolk City League baseball. The Referees' Plaque awarded him by William and Mary in 1965 reflects sportsmanship as well as continuing contributions to area track and field programs. *Courtesy of Sports Information Office*

LOUIS G. PLUMMER

A coach who regularly recruits among high school bandsmen for athletes would seem to be an unlikely candidate himself for a college sports hall of fame, but the unorthodox tactic may be one reason Lou Plummer was inducted in 1981. In one four-year span, his Old Dominion track squads won twenty-eight straight dual meets. They finished first in the Little Eight in 1961, 1962, 1963, and 1964, and second in 1957, 1958, 1959, and 1960. They also were second in the Mason-Dixon Conference in 1963, and third in 1964, 1965, and 1966. The overall dual meet record, 1956-1966, was 55-20. His cross-country teams ruled the Little Eight in 1962, 1963, 1965, and 1966, and topped the Mason-Dixon fields in 1963 and 1965. With all his coaching, Plummer still found time to be the trainer for all Old Dominion teams for a dozen years, teach a full load of academic courses in the Department of Health and Physical Education, and serve three years as director of the university's evening and summer program. *Courtesy of Sports Information Office*

SONNY ALLEN

The coaches who knew Sonny Allen best voted him NABC College Division II National Coach of the Year in 1975 when his "Runnin' Monarchs" won the NCAA Division II basketball championship by defeating New Orleans University, 76-74. The Associated Press also voted him 1975 Small College Coach of the Year. Those coast-to-coast honors capped a remarkable ten year tenure during which he lifted Old Dominion from a 7-17 record playing a mixture of Division III and II opponents to one second-place national finish in Division II in 1971 and then a 25-6 record against Division I and Division II teams and the national title. His charter at Old Dominion, beginning with the 1965-1966 season, had been to field teams worthy of a growing college and a mushrooming multi-city metropolitan area. To achieve that goal, he began granting athletic scholarships to Monarch cagers, a first at the school. Among these athletes were to be Academic All-American Gray Eubank, and first-team AP/UPI/NABC All-Americans Dave Twardzik, Joel Copeland, and Wilson Washington. Before Sonny left Old Dominion for Southern Methodist University at the end of the 1974–1975 championship season, his teams had reached post-season tournaments in six of his last seven seasons. *Courtesy of Sports Information Office*

DAVID TWARDZIK

Dave Twardzik became Old Dominion's initial first-team All-American basketball player after leading the Monarchs to runner-up honors in the 1971 NCAA Division II national championship. Twardzik inspired his teammates to fixty-six victories in three years before going on to spark the Portland Trailblazers to the 1976-1977 championship. In between, the 6'1" guard proved himself in professional basketball with the Virginia Squires. The former Monarch captain, whose number 14 was retired in 1972, passed out 880 assists for a career record here and scored 1,660 points while triggering Old Dominion's fast break attack. He also established career records by making 548 free throws out of 686 attempted. His outstanding passing, aggressive floor play, and pressure shooting earned him berths on Associated Press, United Press International, Basketball News, and National Association of Basketball Coaches All-American teams after the 1971-1972 season. *Courtesy of Sports Information Office*

FREDERICK M. KOVNER

Fred Kovner, the "finest all-around outfielder" at Old Dominion University in at least thirty-two years, twice earned first-team All-American honors before graduating in 1965 with thirteen team records. Fred led the Monarchs to NCAA Eastern championships in 1963 and 1964 and to runner-up honors in 1965. His batting averages of .316, .330, .345, and .415 helped bring All-American recognition in 1964 and 1965 and a Chicago White Sox contract in 1965. Kovner's speed, batting prowess, and powerful arm helped Old Dominion to an 82-17 record during his four years on campus. He appeared destined for a major league career before an automobile injury cut short his professional playing time while he was at Lynchburg in Class A ball. The baseball records owned by Kovner, a math major who also regularly played the cello in the Norfolk Symphony, include: most runs batted in (7) and most hits (5) in one game, most home runs (7) and most consecutive home runs (3) in one season, most consecutive hits (7) and most consecutive times (12) on base, most hits (44) and most runs (31) in a season, most stolen bases (16) and most total bases (72) in a season, most career home runs (15) and total bases (197), and most runs scored (91) in a career. *Courtesy of Sports Information Office*

C. FRED EDMONDS

Fred Edmonds is the only athlete to have lettered in football, basketball, baseball, and track during the first fifty-two years of Old Dominion University's sports history. A halfback and a quarterback in football, a guard in basketball, a pitcher and utilityman in baseball, and a sprinter and a long-jumper in track, Edmonds starred for the Norfolk Division from the fall of 1933 until the fall of 1936. Edmonds also chaired the campus honor council, was vice president of the IMPS Club, and was a member of the publicity board of the campus newspaper, the *High Hat*. He captained both basketball and baseball teams two different years. He led the cagers through the 1933-1934 and 1934-1935 seasons when they earned records of 11-6 and 10-6, and he paced the 1935 and 1936 baseball squads. He was a regular halfback as a sophomore when the Norfolk Division Braves played a schedule that included four-year colleges, freshman teams, and military elevens. The next year he was a quarterback for five games before he left school during the nation's worst depression to take a promising job that turned into a forty-year career with Texaco. *Courtesy of Sports Information Office*

HARRY LOZON

All-American basketball player, Harry Lozon held or shared at least four school records when he graduated in 1970 after leading the Monarchs to a 61-24 record and two regional tournaments. The sharp-shooting, hard-driving 6-3 forward scored 1,424 points and claimed 513 rebounds when Old Dominion was driving upward in national awareness. He was drafted by the San Diego Rockets. Lozon left campus with a season record in field goal percentage (.607 from 215-354 marksmanship in 1967-1968), and a single-game shooting mark of 11-11 in field goals against then RPI on February 14, 1968. He also shared in a team scoring record average of 98.15 points and a team free throw accuracy mark of .742, both set in 1967-1968 by the 19-7 squad. Lozon was named in *Who's Who in American Colleges* and as Old Dominion's outstanding athlete in 1970. He also has served as a Monarch Club president, the first official "Big Blue" mascot, a member of the women's basketball scholarship committee, a volunteer assistant coach with the women's basketball program, and a member of the Intercollegiate Scholarship Committee. *Courtesy of Sports Information Office*

JOEL COPELAND

All-American basketball player Joel Copeland ranked third in all-time scoring and second in all-time rebounding when he graduated in 1974. The 6-7 center-forward set a career record of 838 field goals and a season record of 682 points while helping the Monarchs achieve a combined record of 74-35 and finish second in the 1971 NCAA Division II national championship. A great shooter, a powerful rebounder, and a determined defender, Copeland finished his career with 1,657 points and 939 rebounds. Those varsity totals were achieved in three years plus two games. His single-game scoring high was forty-four points in the 1974 NCAA South Atlantic Regional. A sensational performance with twenty points and twelve rebounds in the 1971 title game, while he was a freshman playing in only his second varsity game, marked him as a future college All-American. He already had earned high school All-American honors while scoring 2,388 points for Southwestern High School in Franklin. He was selected to the first teams of the United Press International and the National Association of Basketball Coaches all-star teams, while also being placed on the Associated Press Little All-American second team. He had been voted to second-team College Division All-American ranks as a junior. *Courtesy of Sports Information Office*

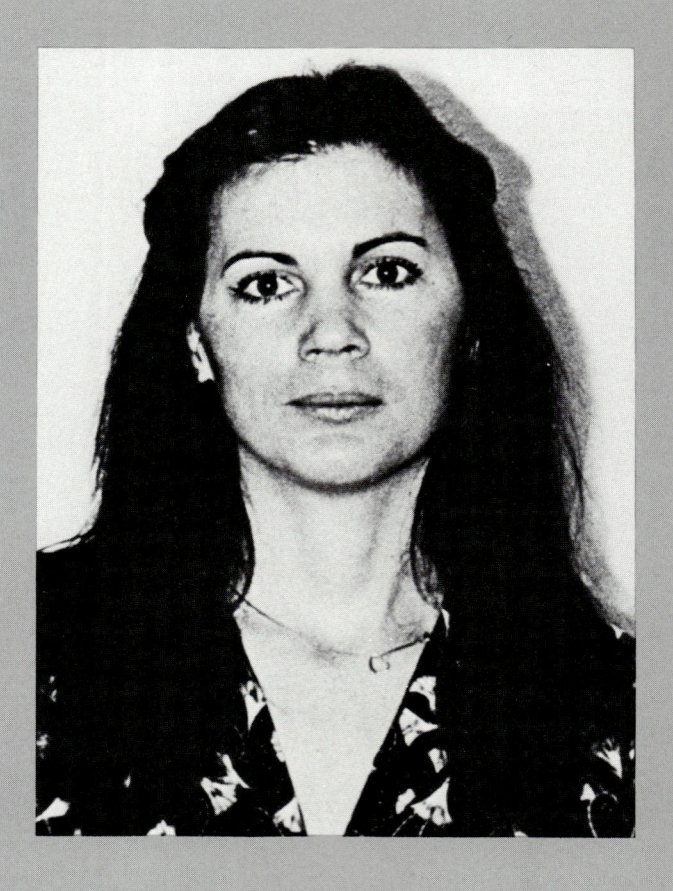

MARY FLEET SUTTON

Mary Fleet Sutton personally outscored women's teams from thirty-six colleges and universities in the national women's swimming meet in 1970. The first woman ever to coach any men's team at Old Dominion, she coached both men and women swimmers after graduating in 1973 with three state swimming records, five Old Dominion marks, and having earned places in six national races. The only woman to have competed for an Old Dominion men's team, Sutton won two varsity letters as a freshman in the 1969-1970 season. She also was named as most outstanding woman swimmer for four straight years. A change in national rules after her freshman year prevented her from continuing to swim on the men's team. She went on to set the state records in the 50-yard and 100-yard butterfly, and 100-yard freestyle. Her school records were in the 50-yard butterfly, 100-yard butterfly, 100-yard individual medley, 100-yard backstroke, and 50-yard freestyle. Her individual points placed Old Dominion fourteenth among fifty colleges and universities competing in the 1970 Association of Intercollegiate Athletics for Women national swimming championship. *Courtesy of Sports Information Office*

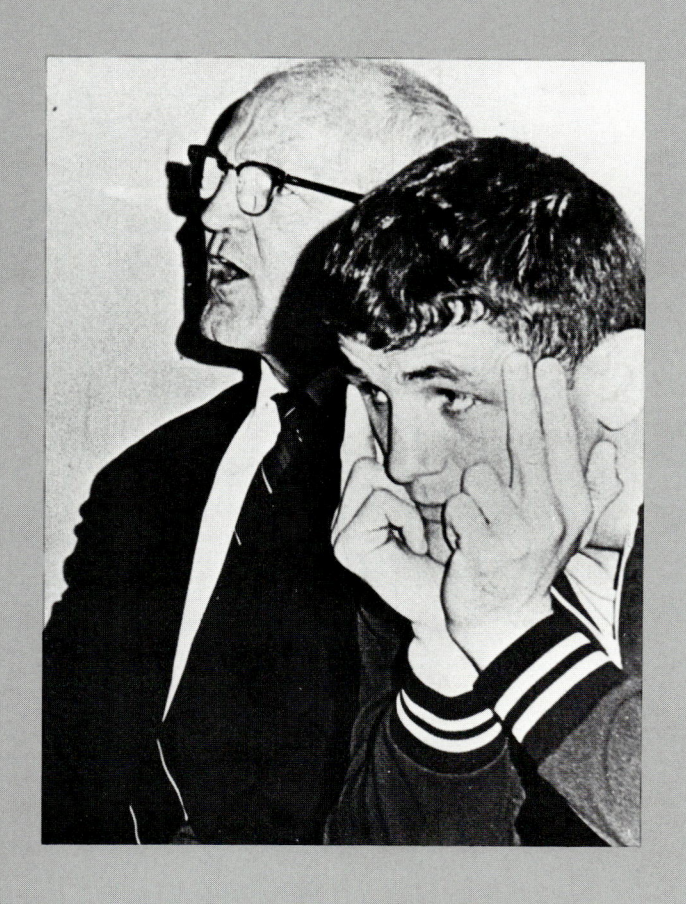

WAYNE BRIGHT

Wayne Bright, shown here with Coach Pete Robinson, became the first Divison I All-American athlete in Old Dominion University's sports history in 1970. Bright, a two-time All-American with a three-year varsity record of 65-11, placed fourth in the NCAA Division I national championship in 1970 after wrestling his way to the NCAA Division II, 142-pound title. He had earned a fifth-place finish in Division II ranks the year before. The legendary Dan Gable of Iowa State University stopped Bright's bid for a double crown in 1970. Bright, whose season marks were 14-2, 26-5, and 25-4, became a college wrestler after starring in football, wrestling, and baseball for Deep Creek High School in Chesapeake. He helped Old Dominion finish sixth nationally in his junior year. Bright was also a member of the 1970 East All-Star squad, a two-time Monarch Open champion, and a three-time Mason-Dixon Conference champion. *Courtesy of Sports Information Office*

ARTHUR B. "BUD" METHENY

Bud Metheny coached baseball and basketball teams that won 638 games and fourteen championships and also served for seven years as athletic director of Old Dominion University. Metheny coached thirty-two baseball teams and seventeen basketball squads on the Old Dominion campus, beginning in 1948 after a professional baseball career that included four years in right field with the New York Yankees. During his seven years as athletic director, the Monarchs began a drive that carried them from a Division III level to NCAA Division I and several national championships. His thirty-two baseball teams captured twenty-seven winning years that included two NCAA Eastern Regional College Division championships, eight Little Eight titles, and four Mason-Dixon championships. His baseball record was 441-369. Three of his players earned All-American honors—Fred Kovner, Bob Walton, and Jimmy Zadell. He was named as NCAA College Division Baseball Coach of the Year in 1965 after being selected as NCAA Eastern Regional Coach of the Year in 1963 and 1964. He coached baseball from the fall of 1948 through the spring of 1980. Metheny's basketball teams began with the 1948-1949 season and ended with the 1964-1965 squad. His basketball record was 197-166. One of his players, Leo Anthony, became the school's first All-American cager following the 1958-1959 season. Bud was athletic director from 1963 to 1970, a time of considerable growth for the metropolitan area and the school. During this time, Old Dominion significantly increased the scope of its sports program and began giving athletic scholarships for the first time. *Courtesy of Sports Information Office*

ROBERT M. WALTON

Bobby Walton twice earned All-American honors while pitching Old Dominion baseball teams to NCAA Eastern Regional College Division championships. He became Old Dominion's first All-American baseball player in 1963 after pitching the Monarchs over the University of Buffalo to a regional title. He was named to the All-American first team after compiling a 7-2 record with an earned run average of 1.41. He repeated as an All-American pitcher in 1964 with a 9-1 record and a 2.48 earned run average after the Monarchs defeated Buffalo and Long Island University for their second straight NCAA Eastern Regional title. Old Dominion baseball records set by Walton include completing eight consecutive games, starting thirty-three games, hurling twenty-one complete games, winning twenty-five victories, throwing twenty-two straight scoreless innings, pitching two consecutive shutouts, and giving up no walks in a nine-inning game. He also shared the lowest team earned run average, a 2.27 mark set in 1964. His seventy-two pitches in nine innings against Buffalo stood for fifteen years. Walton's twenty-five career wins were achieved with a team that earned a four-year record of 78-17. His season marks were 3-3, 6-1, 7-2, and 9-1. *Courtesy of Sports Information Office*

ARTHUR W. SPEAKES, JR.

"Buttons" Speakes, starred in both basketball and baseball after becoming one of the first athletic scholarship students at Old Dominion and the first black athlete to play in the Mason-Dixon Conference. He was named Old Dominion's Athlete of the Year in 1969 at the end of a career during which he scored 1,005 points in basketball, gained all-tournament honors, and earned a professional baseball offer with his play at third base. He captained Old Dominion's freshman basketball team and averaged 18.7 points, with a high of twenty-eight against the Duke frosh. He also became a regular at third base for the baseball team. As a sophomore, the 5-11 guard earned most valuable player honors on the basketball team and scored 12.7 points per game. He also hit .364 on the baseball team. After helping the Monarch cagers finish 19-7 during his junior year, Speakes paced them to two tournament championships and a 21-10 finish during his senior season. They captured the school's first Mason-Dixon Tourney cage title and played in Old Dominion's first NCAA South Atlantic Regional. Earlier, they won the Fort Eustis Invitational. He scored 10.3 points per game as a junior and 14.5 as a senior. *Courtesy of Sports Information Office*

CARL L. RAGLAND, JR.

Carl Ragland became the first national champion ever at Old Dominion when he captured the NCAA College Division 152-pound wrestling title in 1969 and was also named the most outstanding wrestler in that tournament. The national championship capped an exceptional career during which the two-time All-American athlete achieved a three-year varsity record of 89-6-1 and earned eight tournament titles. Ragland won the national championship with five NCAA tournament wins. The last four came by pins in a total of 14.5 minutes and gained him the Gorriaran Award for the most falls in the least time. He was voted Old Dominion's outstanding athlete in 1969, when he received a new trophy established to recognize an exceptional level of achievement. Ragland also was selected as the outstanding Tidewater athlete by the Virginia Beach Sports Club, became a finalist in the Sigma Nu national fraternity's athlete of the year award search, and was listed in the 1969 *Outstanding College Athletes of America. Courtesy of Sports Information Office*

WILSON WASHINGTON

Wilson Washington, a shot-blocking center who inspired the Big Blue to three exceptional years and a national title in 1975, gained the university's first Division I All-American basketball recognition in 1977. An Associated Press Division I honorable mention choice after the 1976-1977 season, a first-team Division II selection following the 1975-1976 campaign, and a third-team Division II pick after playing just half of the 1974-1975 season, he became a second-round pick of the NBA's Philadelphia 76ers. He has also played professionally for the New Jersey Nets and for teams in Italy and Holland. Washington was chosen the most outstanding player in the 1975 NCAA Division II tournament after leading Old Dominion to its first national championship. He also earned MVP honors in the 1975 Kiwanis-Old Dominion Classic and the 1976 NCAA South Atlantic Regional. Team season records that he contributed to included most points (2,683 in 1974-1975), most consecutive wins (22 in 1976-1977), best field goal percentage (.498 in 1976-1977), most field goals (1,140 in 1974-1975), most field goals attempted (2,363 in 1974-1975). His game highs were twelve blocked shots, twenty-four rebounds and twenty-six points. *Courtesy of Sports Information Office*

JEAN HOLLOMAN WHITEHURST

Jean Holloman Whitehurst starred in basketball and field hockey at Old Dominion University and on ten state AAU basketball championship teams. An all-state basketball forward who averaged from fifteen to thirty points per game in college and AAU play, as well as an all-tournament field hockey wing and left inner, Whitehurst has made substantial contributions to the university and its sports programs and to community sports since she graduated with a B.S. in medical technology in 1956. She twice received the outstanding female athlete award at Old Dominion, in 1950 when she earned an A.A. degree and again in 1956 when she was awarded a B.S. degree. She captained the field hockey team in 1949. She received Old Dominion's Alumni Association Service Award in 1980, after serving for twenty years on the Alumni Association board of directors, including terms as vice president and as secretary. *Courtesy of Sports Information Office*

BOBBY C. JAMES

Bobby James set a number of records while he was winning twenty-two state, AAU, and conference championships from 1958 to 1962. Only one-tenth of a second away from qualifying for Olympic competition in 1962 when he raced to a 10.0-second time in the high hurdles in an East Coast AAU meet, James set a Virginia record in 1961 with a 14.3 mark in the State Intercollegiate Meet. The 5'11" athlete also set a 14-1 standard in winning a South Atlantic AAU high hurdle race. Five state indoor and outdoor titles were swept by James while racing for Old Dominion. He also hurdled to four South Atlantic AAU championships, seven Little Eight Conference crowns, and six state AAU wins. He also finished second six times. In addition to excelling in the hurdles, he also competed at times in the long jump, 100-yard dash, and the mile relay for coaches Lou Plummer and Scrap Chandler. This versatility also was apparent in high school, where he once outscored the entire Norview High School track team with points racked up in seven events. He also won a state hurdling title while at Warwick High School in Newport News. *Courtesy of Sports Information Office*

JOHN P. LEIGH III

J. P. Leigh became Old Dominion University's only All-American golfer when he finished fifth in the NCAA Division II national tournament at Albuquerque in 1969, and also finished among the top twenty-five golfers in Division I competition. The three-time Mason-Dixon Conference champion lost only one dual match as a Monarch. A professional from 1969 to 1974, he regained his amateur status in 1977 and had won more than seventy tournaments by 1984. Those wins included the 1983 Eastern Amateur. Twice low amateur in the Virginia PGA Open, he also won six Portsmouth City Amateur tourneys, four MacArthur tournaments, four Suffolk Amateurs, and three Norfolk City Amateurs before he was inducted into the Sports Hall of Fame in 1984. His contributions to Old Dominion athletics have included helping Coach Pete Robinson tutor the golf team, serving for many years as co-chairman with golf coach Murray Rudisill of the Monarch golf scholarship fund, and serving on the golf committee of the Old Dominion University Intercollegiate Foundation.
Courtesy of Sports Information Office

DICK ST. CLAIR

Dick St. Clair was an All-American basketball star who established new standards in passing excellence while captaining three Old Dominion University teams to sixty-one victories. A 5'9" guard who dunked, St. Clair averaged 8.7 assists per game while scoring 1,038 points. He helped pace the 1967-1968 team to a season scoring record of 98.2 points per game and nineteen victories. Old Dominion won twenty-one games each of the next two seasons. "Dick was the first great passing guard I had," said former ODU coach Sonny Allen. "Dave Twardzik and a lot of other fine guards who came after him copied his style. The sign of a good guard is what he does for his teammates. Dick was great at getting the ball to others at the right time. They could play with the confidence that they would get the ball at the right spot and the right time." St. Clair scored 14.4 points per game on the 1967-1968 team, then boosted his average to 17.7 as a junior when he earned All-American honorable mention honors.
Courtesy of Sports Information Office

JAMES W. CLARK III

Jim Clark, who became Old Dominion's first male All-American swimmer in 1973, graduated in 1974 with five individual and three relay records and with eighteen medals won in the Virginia State championships. His records were in the 50-yard, 60-yard, 100-yard, and 200-yard freestyles, in the 400-yard and 800-yard freestyle relays, and the 400-yard medley. The Norfolk Catholic High School graduate, who was a four-sport letterman there, became Old Dominion's first male All-American swimmer by placing eighth in 100-yard freestyle competition in the 1973 NCAA Division II national meet. He also set career and season records for points scored, was selected as the team's most valuable player his junior and senior years, and twice served as team captain. *Courtesy of Sports Information Office*

THOMAS M. "PETE" ROBINSON

Until he retired in 1983, after twenty-six years of coaching Old Dominion University Monarchs, Pete Robinson was the only head wrestling coach in the university's history. During Robinson's career here, Old Dominion became a Division II power and then rose to a well-respected Division I status. Through those years, his teams compiled a 172-133-7 record. During Pete's tenure, fourteen of his teams posted winning seasons with two earning national rankings in 1969 and 1974. His 1981-1982 team won the NCAA East Regionals and sent four wrestlers on to the NCAA national championships. His 1982-1983 team finished second in the regionals after becoming his fourth team to capture the Virginia state title. Pete was honored in March, 1983 at the NCAA national championships by the National Coaches Wrestling Association for his twenty-five years as a college coach. Recognized and respected nationally for his coaching, Robinson also served as a member of the national rules committee of the NCAA and as director for several post-season tournaments. He also coached golf at Old Dominion for thirteen years. One golfer, J. P. Leigh, earned Division II All-American honors in 1969. *Courtesy of Sports Information Office*

TONY ZONTINI

Tony Zontini set state and school records while competing for Old Dominion University's track, baseball, and basketball teams from 1964 through 1968. He lettered four years in indoor track and outdoor track, three years in baseball and two years in basketball during the years when freshmen were not eligible for varsity baseball or basketball. Zontini set the state collegiate indoor low hurdles record in the 1964-1965 season, won Mason-Dixon Conference low hurdle and high hurdle titles, participated in the NCAA Regionals in the high hurdles and intermediate hurdles, and competed in numerous invitational, regional, and NCAA indoor track meets. In outdoor track competition, he also won the Mason-Dixon high and intermediate hurdle titles two straight years, and placed in 100-yard and 220-yard dashes and in the 440-yard and 880-yard relays. He competed in the NCAA Regionals in high hurdles and intermediate hurdles and ran in many other invitational, regional, and NCAA meets. The starting varsity third baseman for three years, he hit .392 as a junior and .352 as a senior. He set or shared school records by hitting two triples in one game and two homers in another. The triple record was still standing after seventeen years when he was inducted into the Sports Hall of Fame. *Courtesy of Sports Information Office*

NANCY LIEBERMAN

Nancy Lieberman, who helped the 1976 U.S. Olympic basketball team win a silver medal and then twice earned college player-of-the-year honors, led the Lady Monarchs to two national championships during her career at Old Dominion University from 1976 to 1980. Three times an All-American selection, the 5'11" guard led Old Dominion teams to a four-year record of 125-15 with a school-record 961 assists, 2,430 points, 1,167 rebounds, and 512 steals. Lieberman paced the Lady Monarchs to a 30-4 record and a National Women's Invitational Tournament title that crowned the 1977-1978 season. The Far Rockaway, New York, native then helped the Lady Monarchs earn Association of Intercollegiate Athletics for Women national championships in both 1979 and 1980. The team's records for those years were 35-1 and 37-1. Her All-American honors included Kodak All-American—1978, 1979, 1980; National Scouting Association All-American, 1979; National Women's Invitational All-American, 1977–1978; most valuable player, First Annual All-American Basketball Classic, 1978; and most valuable player Underalls All-American Classic, 1978. *Courtesy of Sports Information Office*

INGE NISSEN

Inge Nissen, a three-time All-American center from Denmark, scored 2,647 points and claimed 1,459 rebounds while helping the Lady Monarchs win three national basketball championships. The 6'5" center owned most of Old Dominion's scoring and rebounding records when she graduated in 1980 and still was listed with ten of those records when she was inducted into the Sports Hall of Fame in 1985. Nissen helped pace the 1977-1978 team to a 30-4 record and the Lady Monarch's first national title—the National Women's Invitational Tournament championship. She increased her scoring to 22.0 points per game with the 1978-1979 squad that finished 35-1 after claiming an Association of Intercollegiate Athletics for Women national championship. All-American honors included: Kodak All-American, 1980; National Scouting Association All-American, 1979, 1980; and National Women's Invitational Tournament All-American, 1978. She also played in the 1978 and 1979 Underalls All-American Basketball Classic, and the 1978 All-American Basketball Classic. *Courtesy of Sports Information Office*

RONNIE VALENTINE

The first player in NCAA basketball history to score in double figures in more than 100 games (101), Ronnie Valentine set an all-time school scoring record of 2,204 points and became a two-time Associated Press Division I All-American player. As a two-time captain, Valentine led his teammates to an 84-31 record while also finishing as the Monarch's fifth all-time rebounder. He shot fifty-one percent during his career. The 6'7" forward scored 22.4 points and averaged 9.3 rebounds as a freshman on a team that set a state record by winning twenty-two games in a row, beat Georgetown University in an Eastern College Athletic Conference Blue-Gray playoff, and hosted Villanova University in Old Dominion's first National Invitational Tournament (NIT) appearance. That team finished 25-4. His 1978-1979 team beat Wagner and Clemson in NIT play before losing to Purdue in the quarterfinals and ending the season with a 23-7 record. His senior year, the Monarchs finished 25-5 with a loss in NCAA play to a UCLA team that earned second place in that post-season tournament. *Courtesy of Sports Information Office*

Inducted into the Old Dominion University Sports Hall of Fame in 1986 were, from left to right, Michael Valantassis, Paul Cote, George Consolvo, Woody Barnes, and Randy Leddy. Courtesy of Sports Information Office

MIKE VALANTASSIS

Old Dominion's first soccer All-American, Mike Valantassis, a native of Athens, Greece, was selected to the second team by the National Soccer Coaches Association in 1978. He scored nineteen career goals and assisted eleven others. Valantassis was a two-time All-State and All-District pick and in 1978 he was named the Virginia Intercollegiate Soccer Player of the Year. While playing a defensive back position much of the time, Valantassis nevertheless became one of Old Dominion's ranking all-time scorers. In 1977 and 1978, he captained the team and led Old Dominion to a 35-20-3 mark for four seasons, including a 13-2 record in 1975.

PAUL COTE

Paul Cote wrestled at Old Dominion from 1962 to 1966. He compiled a 57-5-1 mark at the 157-pound class. He was a four-time Mason Dixon Conference champion and was voted the most outstanding wrestler in the 1965 Mason Dixon Tournament. During the 1965-1966 season, Cote became the first wrestler to compete in the NCAA College Division Nationals. That year he was named by the Alumni Association as the school's outstanding athlete. A 1962 graduate of Norfolk Catholic High School, he is a vice president account supervisor with a leading New York stock brokerage house.

GEORGE CONSOLVO

One of Virginia's top collegiate tennis players, George Consolvo captured the NCAA Eastern Region College Division singles championship in 1966 and 1967. He was a four-year letterman and compiled a 43-17 record. Consolvo was named the team's most valuable player in both 1966 and 1967. He was the recipient of the Tom Scott Award in 1967 and the winner of the WTAR award given to the athlete with the highest academic average in 1967. A 1963 graduate of Maury High School in Norfolk, Consolvo is a partner in the Norfolk law firm of Kaufman and Canoles. He was awarded two bronze stars and two Army commendation medals while performing military service from 1967 to 1971.

WOODY BARNES

Woody Barnes played football, basketball, and baseball at the Norfolk Division from 1935 to 1938. In football, Barnes played end and quarterback. He led the Norfolk Division to an 8-1 record in 1935, which included a 7-4 victory over the William and Mary freshmen. He also played in the first night game at Foreman Field against Louisburg College. A forward on the basketball team, Barnes led the team to a 15-4 mark in 1937-1938 and a 34-18 mark during his three-year career. Barnes, who was an outstanding pitcher in baseball, was named the most outstanding athlete in the Tidewater area of Virginia in 1937.

RANDY LEDDY

Randy Leddy was the most prolific basketball rebounder in Old Dominion history, capturing 1,153 rebounds during his four-year career. He is also one of only three Monarchs to grab over one thousand rebounds and score over one thousand points. Leddy is ranked high on Old Dominion's all-time scoring list with 1,411 points. A four-year letterman, Leddy was named the team's most valuable player for three consecutive years. In 1966, he was named Honorable Mention-Little All-American and in that same season averaged an Old Dominion school record of 18.1 rebounds per game. Leddy played under both coaches Bud Metheny and Sonny Allen, and with Fred Edmonds, Jr., co-captained the team during the 1965-1966 season.

Appendix A

In 1947, Lewis W. Webb, Jr., director of the Norfolk Division of the College of William and Mary, created the Advisory Board. This board served as a connection between the community and the Norfolk Division to provide Director Webb with a better understanding of the community's needs and how the Norfolk Division of the College of William and Mary could best serve them. The Advisory Board exercised local authority, as it was granted by the director, however, the Board of Visitors of the College of William and Mary was the legal governing body of the Norfolk Division.

In 1962, an act of the Virginia General Assembly separated the Norfolk Division from the parent institution. The commonwealth of Virginia authorized the Norfolk Division to operate as an independent state institution governed by its own Board of Visitors. The Board of Visitors adopted the name Old Dominion College for the new institution and in 1969 it became Old Dominion University.

The Board of Visitors was originally composed of thirteen members appointed to a four-year term by the governor of Virginia. The number of members grew in 1980 to seventeen. Each member may serve two consecutive four-year terms. The Board of Visitors is annually required to meet at the school at least once. The members choose from among themselves a rector, vice rector, and a secretary. These appointments are for two years and board members may serve up to four terms of office.

The Virginia General Assembly granted the following authority to the Old Dominion University Board of Visitors: "The board shall make all needful rules and regulations concerning the University, appoint the president, who shall be its chief executive officer, and all professors, teachers, staff members, and agents, and fix their salaries, and generally direct the affairs of the University." (Code of Virginia 23-49.17)

The members of the Advisory Board and the Board of Visitors are listed below chronologically:

Advisory Board, 1947—John S. Alfriend, E. S. Brinkley, Forest F. Cathey, E. T. Gresham, C. A. Harrell, Charles L. Kaufman, Henry S. Lewis, Abner S. Pope, Crawford S. Rogers, J. Hoge Tyler III, Nick Wright.

Advisory Board, 1948—E. S. Brinkley, Rev. T. F. Carroll, F. F. Cathey, E. T. Gresham, L. W. I'Anson, H. S. Lewis, A. S. Pope, C. S. Rogers.

Advisory Board, 1950—John S. Alfriend, E. S. Brinkley, Joseph S. Johnston, Rabbi Louis D. Mendoza, John Twohy II, E. T. Gresham, L. W. I'Anson, C. L. Kaufman, Abner S. Pope, J. Hoge Tyler III.

Advisory Board, 1951—Same members as 1950.

Advisory Board, 1952—J. S. Alfriend, J. J. Brewbaker, E. T. Gresham, L. W. L'Anson, C. L. Kaufman, Rabbi L. D. Mendoza, A. S. Pope, John Twohy II, J. H. Tyler III.

Advisory Board, 1953—J. S. Alfriend, J. J. Brewbaker, E. T. Gresham, L. W. L'Anson, C. L. Kaufman, Rabbi L. D. Mendoza, John Twohy II, J. H. Tyler III.

Advisory Board, 1954—J. S. Alfriend, J. J. Brewbaker, A. B. Clarke, E. T. Gresham, L. W. L'Anson, C. L. Kaufman, A. S. Pope, John Twohy II, J. H. Tyler III.

Advisory Board, 1955—J. S. Alfriend, J. J. Brewbaker, L. W. L'Anson, Edward H. Jones, C. S. Kaufman, S. C. Lampert, Abner S. Pope, Rabbi Malcolm H. Stern, John Twohy, II, J. H. Tyler III.

Advisory Board, 1956—J. S. Alfriend, Frank Batten, J. J. Brewbaker, E. T. Gresham, L. W. L'Anson, C. L. Kaufman, S. C. Lampert, W. Peyton May, Abner S. Pope, J. H. Tyler III

Advisory Board, 1957—J. S. Alfriend, Frank Batten, J. J. Brewbaker, Roy S. Charles, Pretlow Darden, E. T. Gresham, Henry Clay Hofheimer II, C. L. Kaufman, S. C. Lampert, William T. McMillan, W. Peyton May, Abner S. Pope, Toy D. Savage, John G. Sellers, J. H. Tyler III.

Advisory Board, 1958—J. S. Alfriend, A. C. Bartlett, Frank Batten, J. J. Brewbaker, Roy R. Charles, Pretlow Darden, E. T. Gresham, Henry Clay Hofheimer II, C. L. Kaufman, S. C. Lampert, William T. McMillan, W. Peyton May, Abner S. Pope, Toy D. Savage, Jr., John G. Sellers, J. H. Tyler III.

Advisory Board, 1959-1961—J. S. Alfriend, A. C. Bartlett, Frank Batten, J. J. Brewbaker, A. D. Chandler, Roy R. Charles, Pretlow Darden, E. T. Gresham, Henry Clay Hofheimer II, C. L. Kaufman, S. C. Lampert, William T. McMillan, W. Peyton May, Abner S. Pope, Toy D. Savage, Jr., John G. Sellers, J. H. Tyler III.

The Board of Visitors' year begins on July 1 and ends on June 30. Other officers of the board will be identified in the year by year listings of the board members by the following symbols: *VR* for vice rector and *S* for secretary.

Board of Visitors, 1962-1963—Joseph E. Baker, Frank Batten, Roy R. Charles, Charles B. Cross, Jr., Thomas N. Downing, Darden W. Jones, James A. Howard—*S*, Mrs. Harvey Lindsay, W. Peyton May—*VR*, Mrs. John F. Rixey, A. K. Scribner, Sr., Reid M. Spencer, James W. Wood.

Board of Visitors, 1963-1964, 164-1965, 1965-1966—Same as 1962-1963.

Board of Visitors, 1966-1967—Joseph E. Baker, Frank Batten, Charles B. Cross, Jr., Thomas N. Downing, James A. Howard—*S*, Darden W. Jones, Mrs. Harvey Lindsay, W. Peyton May—*VR*, Robert L. Payne, Jr., Mrs. John F. Rixey, A. K. Scribner, Sr., Reid M. Spencer, James W. Wood.

Board of Visitors, 1967-1968—Same as 1966-1967.

Board of Visitors, 1968-1969—Frank Batten, Thomas P. Chisman, Edwin W. Chittum, Francis N. Crenshaw, James A.

Howard—*S*, Mrs. Harvey Lindsay, J. Henry McCoy, Jr., W. Peyton May—*VR*, Reid M. Spencer, A. E. S. Stephens, A. K. Scribner, James W. Roberts, Robert L. Payne, Jr.

Board of Visitors, 1969-1970—Same as 1968-1969.

Board of Visitors, 1970-1971—Frank Batten, Thomas P. Chisman, Edwin W. Chittum, Francis N. Crenshaw, Edgar S. Everhart, Albert B. Gornto, Jr.—*VR*, James A. Howard, Mrs. George M. Kaufman, Wayne Lustig, J. Henry McCoy, Jr., Milton A. Reid, James W. Roberts, A. E. S. Stephens.

Board of Visitors, 1971-1972—Frank Batten, Thomas P. Chisman, Edwin W. Chittum, Francis N. Crenshaw, Edgar S. Everhart, Albert B. Gornto, Jr.—*VR*, Mrs. George M. Kaufman, Wayne Lustig, J. Henry McCoy, Jr., Kenneth A. Randall, Milton A. Reid, Robert H. Spilman, Joseph L. Yon.

Board of Visitors, 1972-1973—Francis N. Crenshaw—*R*, Albert B. Gornto, Jr.—*VR*, Frank Batten, Bruce T. Bishop, Mrs. Robert G. Doumar, Edgar S. Everhart, Mrs. George M. Kaufman, Wayne Lustig, J. Henry McCoy, Jr., Kenneth A. Randall, Milton A. Reid, Robert H. Spilman, Joseph L. Yon.

Board of Visitors, 1973-1974—Bruce T. Bishop, Francis N. Crenshaw, Mrs. Robert G. Doumar, Edgar S. Everhart, Robert L. Fodrey, Albert B. Gornto, Jr.—*VR*, Mrs. George M. Kaufman, Wayne Lustig, J. Henry McCoy, Jr., Kenneth A. Randall, Robert H. Spilman, Herman E. Valentine, Joseph L. Yon.

Board of Visitors, 1974-1975—Same as 1974.

Board of Visitors, 1976-1977—Bruce T. Bishop, Mrs. Robert G. Doumar, Edgar S. Everhart, Robert L. Fodrey, Albert B. Gornto, Jr.,—*VR*, Carroll F. Harris, Jr., Phillip F. Hudson, Mrs. George M. Kaufman, Wayne Lustig, Shannon T. Mason, Jr., Robert L. Spilman, Herman E. Valentine.

Board of Visitors, 1977-1978—Bruce T. Bishop, Mrs. Robert G. Doumar, Edgar S. Everhart, Robert L. Fodrey, Albert B. Gornto, Jr., Mrs. George F. Kaufman, Wayne Lustig, Shannon T. Mason, Jr., Hon. Walter A. Page, John R. Sears, Jr., Robert H. Spilman, Herman E. Valentine, Joseph L. Yon.

Board of Visitors, 1978-1979—V. M. Annas, Bruce T. Bishop, Dorothy Doumar, Robert L. Fodrey, Kenneth V. Geroe, Shannon T. Mason, Jr., Hon. Walter A. Page, M. Lee Payne, Michael C. Savvides, John R. Sears, Jr., Robert H. Spilman, Herman E. Valentine, Joseph L. Yon.

Board of Visitors, 1979-1980—V. M. Annas, Bruce T. Bishop, Dorothy Doumar, Robert L. Fodrey, Kenneth V. Geroe, Shannon T. Mason, Jr., Mrs. William Old, Hon. Walter A. Page, M. Lee Payne, Michael C. Savvides, John R. Sears, Jr., Herman E. Valentine, Robert W. Wentz, Jr.

Board of Visitors, 1980-1981—Dorothy Doumar—*R*, V. M. Annas, Sonya Bell, Bruce T. Bishop, Andrew Donnelly, Kenneth Geroe, Shannon T. Mason, Mary Sue Neal, John R. Sears, Jr., Robert M. Stanton, Robert Wentz, Jr., M. Lee Payne, J. M. Irby, Michael Savvides.

Board of Visitors, 1981-1982—Dorothy Doumar—*R*, V. M. Annas, Sonya Bell, Bruce T. Bishop, Andrew J. Donnelly, Louis B. Fine, Kenneth V. Geroe, John W. Holsinger, J. M. H. Irby, Shannon T. Mason, Jr., Mary Sue Neal, Sylvia H. Old, M. Lee Payne, Michael C. Savvides, John R. Sears, Jr., Robert M. Stanton, Robert W. Wentz, Jr.

Board of Visitors, 1982-1983—M. Lee Payne—*R*, Sonya Bell, Bruce T. Bishop, Dorothy M. Doumar, Louis B. Fine, Kenneth V. Geroe, John W. Holsinger, J. M. H. Irby, Shannon T. Mason, Mary Sue Neal, Sylvia H. Old, Gammiel G. Poindexter, Michael C. Savvides, John R. Sears, Robert M. Stanton, Joyce Strelitz, Eugene Walters.

Board of Visitors, 1983-1984—M. Lee Payne—*R*, Sonya Bell, George Dragas, Jr., Louis B. Fine, Kenneth V. Geroe, John W. Holsinger, Ann Kilgore, Shannon T. Mason, Jr., Mary Sue Neal, Sylvia H. Old, Gammiel Poindexter, H. B. Price III, Michael C. Savvides, John R. Sears, Jr., Robert M. Stanton, Joyce Strelitz, Eugene Walters.

Board of Visitors, 1984-1985—Robert M. Stanton—*R*, George Dragas, Jr., Kenneth Geroe, James K. Hall, John W. Holsinger, J. William Howell, Ann Kilgore, Beverley R. Lawler, Mary Sue Neal, Sylvia H. Old, M. Lee Payne, Gammiel Poindexter, H. B. Price III, Michael C. Savvides, Joyce Strelitz, Eugene Walters, Charles B. Whitehurst.

Board of Visitors, 1985-1986—Robert M. Stanton—*R*, Richard F. Barry III, George Dragas, Jr., Kenneth V. Geroe, James K. Hall, J. William Howell, Ann Kilgore, Beverley R. Lawler, Arnold B. McKinnon, Laurie Naismith, Sylvia H. Old, Gammiel Poindexter, H. B. Price III, Michael C. Savvides, Joyce Strelitz, Eugene Walters, Charles B. Whitehurst.

Board of Visitors, 1986-1987—Robert M. Stanton—*R*, Richard F. Barry III, George Dragas, Jr., James K. Hall, J. William Howell, Ann Kilgore, Beverley R. Lawler, Arnold H. Leon, Arnold B. McKinnon, R. G. Moore, Laurie Naismith, Sylvia H. Old, Gammiel Poindexter, H. B. Price III, Joyce Strelitz, Eugene Walters, Charles B. Whitehurst.

Appendix B
Eminent Professors

"A select number of full professors may be honored as eminent professors. Procedures for designation shall be the same as those for promotion to full professor.... Departments nominating candidates for eminent professorships will be expected to demonstrate that the nominees have achieved national recognition in their fields and provide supporting evidence. In most cases, this national recognition should be attested by appropriate criteria including expert external opinion. In addition, the candidates must meet the standards established for eminent scholars by the State Council of Higher Education." (1985-1986 Old Dominion University Faculty Handbook)

James L. Bugg, Jr., History

Dwight W. Allen, Arts and Letters

Lewis S. Ford, Philosophy

Ransom Baine Harris, Philosophy

Leonard I. Ruchelman, Urban Studies and Public Administration

Alf J. Mapp, Jr., English

Anne Scott Daughtrey, Management

Betty H. Yarborough, Educational Curriculum and Instruction

Franklin Ross Jones, Educational Leadership and Service

Melvin H. Williams, Health, Physical Education, and Recreation

Surendra N. Tiwari, Mechanical Engineering and Mechanics

Robert L. Ash, Mechanical Engineering and Mechanics

Harold G. Marshall, Biological Sciences

Daniel E. Sonenshine, Biological Sciences

William D. Lakin, Mathematical Sciences

John Tweed, Mathematical Sciences

William M. Dunstan, Oceanography

Wynford L. Harries, Physics

Govind S. Khandelwal, Physics

Albert S. Glickman, Psychology

Richard T. Cheng, Computer Science

Chester E. Grosch, Oceanography

John C. Ludwick, Oceanography

Anthony J. Provenzano, Jr., Oceanography

Ram C. Dahiya, Mathematical Sciences

Frederick W. Culpepper, Jr., Vocational and Technical Education

Larry P. Atkinson, Oceanography

Heinz K. Meier, History

Helen Yura, Nursing

Kurt Maly, Computer Science

Michele M. Darby, Dental Hygiene

William D. Stanley, Electrical Engineering Technology

Appendix C
Faculty Emeriti

The title "emeritus" may be granted only by the Board of Visitors to full-time faculty members "who are retiring in the ranks of professor and associate professor and who have served the university for a period of not less than ten years consecutively prior to retirement" or to "administrative officers who hold faculty rank and tenure" and who have served the university for a period of ten consecutive years prior to retirement. An appointment as an emeritus faculty member carries with it a wide range of privileges and responsibilities.

Name	Years	Rank
Lewis W. Webb, Jr.	1932-1974	President
Lee M. Klinefelter	1942-1959	Professor
Joseph C. Chandler	1942-1969	Professor
W. Herman Bell	1957-1970	Professor
T. Ross Fink	1954-1970	Professor
Ruth F. Harrell	1955-1970	Professor
W. Gerald Akers	1931-1972	Professor
Rogers D. Whichard	1948-1972	Professor
Helen L. Perry	1956-1972	Associate Professor
Yates Stirling III	1948-1972	Associate Professor
Arthur C. Munyan	1961-1973	Professor
Andrew C. Tunyogi	1958-1973	Professor
Melvin A. Pittman	1967-1974	Dean
Edward L. White	1932-1974	Professor
E. Vernon Peele	1948-1975	Dean
Vance E. Grover	1946-1975	Professor
Louis G. Plummer	1956-1975	Professor
Jacques S. Zaneveld	1959-1975	Professor
John E. Baker	1971-1976	Professor
Reuben Cooper	1946-1976	Professor
William J. Hanna	1967-1976	Professor
Emily V. Pittman	1950-1976	Professor
A. Rufus Tonelson	1966-1976	Professor
Charles E. Vogan	1950-1976	Professor
Dorothy Mae Jones	1954-1976	Associate Professor
P. Stephen Barna	1966-1977	Professor
Thomas Blossom	1964-1977	Professor
William W. Seward, Jr.	1945-1977	Professor
Calder S. Sherwood III	1939-1977	Professor
Robert L. Stern	1945-1978	Professor
Ralph F. de Bedts	1960-1979	Eminent Professor
E. Grant Meade	1965-1979	Eminent Professor
Clifford L. Adams	1958-1979	Professor
William M. Beck, Jr.	1946-1979	Professor
Parker Lesley	1959-1979	Professor
Margaret C. Phillips	1943-1979	Professor
Clifford C. Saunders	1961-1979	Professor
Elizabeth S. de Bedts	1959-1979	Associate Professor
Carl N. Helwig	1968-1979	Associate Professor
David E. Delzell	1959-1980	Professor
William E. Hopkins	1962-1980	Professor
Arthur B. Metheny	1948-1980	Professor
Ernest L. Rhodes	1960-1980	Professor
Charles K. Sibley	1955-1980	Professor
Wayne E. Bowman	1955-1980	Associate Professor
David E. Henderson	1965-1981	Professor
Ole S. Johnson	1969-1981	Professor
James B. Reece	1952-1981	Professor
Benjamin F. Clymer, Jr.	1960-1981	Associate Professor
William H. Patterson	1961-1981	Associate Professor
Louis Searleman	1970-1981	Associate Professor
Gene W. Hirschfeld	1967-1982	Eminent Professor
Joseph M. Tyrrell	1959-1982	Professor
Thomas Jackson Reed	1957-1982	Associate Professor
William C. Riesenberg	1970-1982	Associate Professor
Adrienne D. Schellings	1965-1982	Associate Professor

Conrad S. Wilson, Jr.	1955-1982	Associate Professor	John E. MacCormack	1964-1985	Professor
Pauline K. Wise	1963-1982	Associate Professor	Stanley R. Pliska	1946-1985	Professor
Earl C. Kindle	1971-1983	Eminent Professor	Virginia S. Bagley	1945-1985	Associate Professor
Dwight H. Newell	1972-1984	Eminent Professor	Elizabeth S. Henry	1950-1985	Associate Professor
Richard H. Bigelow	1964-1984	Professor	S. Eliot Breneiser	1951-1986	Professor
Edgar A. Kovner	1946-1984	Professor	Charles M. Dehority	1966-1986	Professor
Wendell E. Malbon	1969-1984	Professor	Dorothy E. Johnson	1961-1986	Associate Professor
Joseph P. Mooney	1974-1984	Professor	Ralph V. Lahaie	1966-1985	Professor
Albert I. Godden	1949-1984	Associate Professor	Gennaro L. Goglia	1964-1986	Professor
Henry H. Schmoele, Jr.	1967-1984	Associate Professor	Elbridge K. Reid	1965-1985	Associate Professor
Gerald W. Thompson	1972-1984	Associate Professor	J. Albert Tatem, Jr.	1960-1985	Associate Professor
Frank W. Billmyer, Jr.	1950-1985	Professor	Allan Owen	1961-1986	Associate Professor

Appendix D

Student government at the university has undergone many changes since the 1930s. During the 1940s and '50s, the Student Senate grew to 16 members. In 1958, the Student Government Association created a three-tiered student government with an Executive Council, a Student Council and a Judicial Branch. In fall, 1969, President James L. Bugg, Jr. called for the creation of a university senate which would have students, faculty and administrators in one governing body. By 1970, the Student Caucus became an integral part of the UniSenate. Nine years later, the University Senate was abandoned in favor of a return to an independent Student Senate. Each spring a president, two vice presidents and 30 senators are elected by constituents in their respective colleges.

Student Senate Presidents

Bill Foster, 1961

Robert Padgett, 1962

Anne Haste, 1963

Jack Allbritton, 1964

Bob Fentress, 1965

Errol Donahue, 1966

Bob Deaton, 1967

Ray Dezern, 1968

Gene Woolard, 1969

John Suhre, 1970

John Sasser, 1971

Wallace Gene Haislip, 1972

Bruce Bishop, 1973

Bruce Bishop, 1974

Howard Leader, 1975

Larry Stepp, 1976

Karen Scherberger, 1977

Mike Pitchford, 1978

Bob Burden, 1979

Gordon McDougall, 1980

Rickey Adams, 1981

Keith Curtis, 1982

Keith Curtis, 1983

Karen Gifuni, 1984

Winnie McLean, 1985

R. J. Hixson, 1986

Theodore Hoppe, 1987

Index

A
AROTC 90
Administration Building, New 29
Administration Building, Old 17, 18
Advisory Board 192
Akers, W. Gerald 46
Alfriend Chemistry Building 24, 25
Alfriend, John S. 24, 25, 29
Allen, Sonny 148, 149, 150, 151, 179
Alumni Presidents 68
Ames, Milton B., Jr. 70
Anthony, Leo 178
Aqua Fantasia 106

B
Bagley, Richard 42
Baliles, Gerald M. 63
Baptist Student Center 138
Barnes, Woody 191
Baseball 154-157
Basil, Sophia 173
Basketball, Men's 148-152
Basketball, Women's 144-147
Batten Arts and Letters Bldg. 28, 29
Batten, Frank 22, 28, 34, 35
Bearse, Kevin 157
Bell, W. Herman 52
Bishop, Bruce 40
Blackwater Preserve 40, 60
Board of Visitors 192-193
Bray, Robert 63
Breneiser, S. Eliot 66, 104
Bright, Wayne 183
Brown, John 160, 178
Bud's Emporium 19, 47, 129
Bugg, James L., Jr. 31, 40, 44, 61
Burgess, Charles O. 61
Burruss, Julian A. 45
Button, Robert Y. 37

C
Campus Capers 104
Center for Technology 13
Center for World Trade 63
Chandler, Alvin D. 21
Chandler Hall 21
Chandler, J.A.C. 21, 36, 45, 50
Chandler, Joseph C. Scrap 160, 166, 177
Charity, Bessie 47
Cheerleaders 171-173
Child Study Center 25
Clark, James W. III 188
Clymer, Benjamin F., Jr. 54
Coffey, Harry S. Kit 73
Concert Series 109
Consolvo, George 191
Cootes, Betty S. 114
Copeland, Joel 182
Cote, Paul 191
Crenshaw, Francis N. 40, 41
Cross Country Track 161, 162

D
Daley, Kenneth G. 66
Dalton, John 127
Darby, Michelle M. 63
Darden, Colgate W., Jr. 27, 35, 38
Darden, Constance 27
Darden School of Education 27
Davis, Richard 63
Davis, Ronnie 158
Delta Omega Phi 83, 98
Dental Hygiene Program 26, 63
Dicklin, Paul 108
Dismal Swamp Preserve 89
Distinguished Alumni 70-72
Dixon, Medina 147
Donovan, Anne 147
Dormitory Life 139-141
Dorroh, John H., Jr. 42
Doumar, Dorothy 40
Downing, Thomas N. 39
Duckworth Memorial Hall 28, 33, 37, 57
Duckworth, William Frederick 28, 37
Duke, Charles J. 48
Duncan, Cynthia B. 61

E
ECOS 89
Edmonds, Fred C. 181
Eisenbeiss, William 61
Eminent Professors 194
Etheredge, Samuel N. 72
Everhart, Edgar S. 40

F
Faculty and Staff, 1954-1986 49-65
Faculty Emeriti 59, 195-196
Faculty, 1942 48
Faculty Trio 59
Faculty Wives Club 58
Fahey, John A. 67
Fine Arts Building 20
Fink's Flats 27, 31
Fink, T. Ross 27, 51
First Graduating Class, 1956 83
Fodrey, Robert L., Sr. 35, 71, 73
Football 153
Foreman, A. H. 18, 36
Foreman Field 17, 18, 107
Fortunato, Ronald 75
Fountain of Organized Labor 30
Free University 122

G
Gamma Gamma 96, 97
Gattison, Kenny 152
Gerber, Henry H. 75
Godwin Life Sciences Bldg. 31, 32
Godwin, Mills E., Jr. 21, 32, 37, 70
Goglia, Gennaro L. 67
Golf 170
Gooding, Mike 129
Gornto, Albert B., Jr. 72, 97
Gray's Pharmacy 16

197

Greek Rock 102
Gresham, Earl T. 38
Gresham Hall 24, 29, 38, 141
Gwathmey, Edward 47
Gymnastics 170

H
HACE 60, 62
Hamilton, Norma 55
Hampton Boulevard 16
Harrison, Albertis S. 37
Haws, Charles H. 66
Health and P.E. Building 28
Healy, Joseph E. 36
Henry, Louis H. 66
High Hat 126
Hinderliter, Marie 171
Hirschfeld, Gene W. 63
Hodges, William T. 48
Hofheimer Art Library 20
Hofheimer, Elise N. 20, 35
Hofheimer, Henry Clay II 35, 40
Holland, Margaret B. 68
Holton, Linwood 39
Howell, Henry E., Jr. 71
Hughes Library 20, 22
Hughes, Robert Morton 20, 36

I
Imps 52, 95, 96, 102
Instructional Development 20, 94
International Jubilee 120
International Programs 61
Intramurals 174

J
Jackson, Perry Y. 46
John's College Restaurant 23

K
Kabler, James H. III 74
Kaufman, Charles L. 22, 31, 33, 35
Kaufman Engineering Hall 22, 33
Kaufman, George and Linda 31, 35, 40
Kaufman Mall 23, 31, 102, 136
Kersey, Katherine C. 67
Kilgore, Anne H. 70
King, Rev. Martin L., Jr. 135
Kirby, Raymond H. 67
Kirsch, Bernard 43
Klinefelter, Lee M. 48, 53
Kovner, Edgar A. 73
Kovner, Frederick M. 180
Krasnow, Jeff 151
Krepshaw, Denise 162

L
Lacrosse 169
Lampe, Harold J. 22
Larchmont School, New 14, 18
Larchmont School, Old 12, 14, 18, 19, 82
Lawless, Lawrence C. 74
Leddy, Randy 191

Lee, Buddy 159
Lee, Wiley 157
Leigh, J. P. III 187
Lieberman, Nancy 146, 147, 189
Light Infantry Blues 15
Lindsay, Mr. and Mrs. H. L. 37
Literary Festival 112
Lozon, Harry 181
Ludwig, John 40

M
Mace and Crown 23, 117, 129
Manning, Cleaves L. 41, 72
Mansbach, Harry H. 35, 43
Mapp, Alf J., Jr. 72
Marchello, Joseph M. 11, 44, 61, 62
Marshall, Harold G. 67
Marshall, Mr. and Mrs. C. 37
Martin, Roy B., Jr. 25, 40, 70
Mason, Shannon T., Jr. 73
McClelland, Robert C. 47
McDougall, Gordon 68, 125
Meier, Heinz K. 61
Metheny, Arthur B. 50, 148, 183
Moore, R. G. 43
Moss, Thomas W., Jr. 41
Mullin, Gail 42
Murden, Forrest D., Jr. 70
Musselman, Lytton J. 40

N
NROTC 90
NASA 13, 57, 62, 70
Nettles, T. Earl 73
Newman, Mark 154, 156
Newsom, Tommy 74
Nissen, Inge 147, 190
Norfolk Scope 150

O
Oman, Sidney 86
Oyster Bowl Parade 113

P
Palmer, Warren 39
Paul, Audrey T. Bud 47
Payne, M. Lee 42
Peele, E. Vernon 37
Peninsula Graduate Center 33
Phi Theta Kappa 84
Pi Kappa Alpha 103
Pi Phi Sigma 83, 97, 102
Pickett, Owen B. 41
Piette, J. M. 40
Pliska, Stanley R. 52
Plummer, Louis G. 160, 179
Polson, Beth 74
Pretlow Planetarium 59
Public Safety Building 32

Q
Quirk, Raymond L., Jr. 52

R
Ragland, Carl L., Jr.   185
Ramsey, John W.   55
Rathskeller   140
Reagan, Ronald   146
Rehearsal Hall   15
Reid, Rev. Milton A.   40
Riverview Theater   108
Robb, Charles S.   61, 63
Roberts, Col. James W.   22
Robinson, Thomas Pete   158, 188
Rogers Hall   24, 29, 139
Rollins, Alfred B., Jr.   35, 41, 44, 57, 60, 61, 88, 146

S
Sailing   168
Save ODU Campaign   128, 133
Science Building   18, 19, 129
Scott, Thomas L.   46, 154, 176
Sears, John R., Jr.   41
Seward, William W.   49
Shaw, Artie   113
Shelton, Deborah   75
Shufflebarger, David T.   42
Sibley, Charles K.   51, 88
Slover, Fay Martin   34
Smith, Donna Doyle   177
Soccer   165
Social Studies Building   18
Sonenshine, Daniel E.   67
Speakes, Arthur W., Jr.   184
Spencer, Reid M.   40
Spong, William B., Jr.   40
St. Clair, Dick   187
Stanaway, Norval R.   60, 138
Stanley, Marianne   146
Stanton, Robert M.   61, 62, 63, 72, 86, 146
Staples, M. Marceline   53
Staples, Marceline G.   53
Stern, Robert L.   37, 55, 82
Student Life   78-141
Student Life: Academe   78-94
Student Life: Cultural   109-112
Student Life: General   130-141
Student Life: Leaders   126-129, 196
Student Life: Performances   104-108
Student Life: Protests   122-125
Student Life: Social Clubs   95-103
Student Life: Special Events   113-121
Superdance for M.D.   119
Sutton, Mary Fleet   182
Swimming   166

T
TKE   103
Taback, Israel   62
Tanner, Charles   57
Technical Institute   18, 26, 53
Tennis   167
The Nature Conservancy   40
Theta Xi   102
Thomas, Carolyn   76
Thompson, Robert   76

Tiga   97, 101
Timmerman, H. Edgar   46
Tonelson, A. Rufus   58, 66, 67, 71, 136, 154, 176
Track and Field   160-162
Tri-K   98, 99, 100, 115
Tunyogi, Andrew C.   55
Twardzik, David   188
Tyler, S. Heth   36

U
Union Camp Corporation   40
University Library   31
University Medal   35

V
Valantassis, Mike   191
Valentine, Ronnie   152, 190
Vincent, Patricia   71

W
WMTI-FM   118
WODU   118
Walker, Stanley C.   41
Walters, Gene   43
Walton, Robert M.   184
Washington, Wilson   185
Webb Center   23, 24, 30, 118, 124, 128
Webb, Lewis W., Jr.   21, 23, 35, 37, 39, 44, 45, 46, 47, 48, 71, 86, 90
Webb, Paul   148, 150
Webb, Virginia R.   35, 55
West, Mark   152
Wheeler, Mary Elizabeth   74
White, Edward L.   46
White, Marcia   172
White, Rebecca O.   52
Whitehurst, G. William   7, 37, 39, 51
Whitehurst, Jean Holloman   73, 145, 186
Wilkins, Jack R.   71
Will, Donald   73
Williams, Mel   162
Williamsburg Lawn   18
Women's Center   58
Women's Field Hockey   163-164
Wrestling   158-159
Wright, Harold J.   52

Y
Young Democrats   126
Young Republicans   127
Young, Tom   148, 150

Z
Zaneveld, Jacques   54
Zentz, Bob   107
Zontini, Tony   189
Zumwalt, Elmo   39

About the Authors

John W. Kuehl is chairman of the history department at Old Dominion University. He did undergraduate work at St. Olaf College and earned his M.A. and Ph.D. at the University of Wisconsin. His research interests are in the Early National period of American history and the history of American thought. He began teaching at Old Dominion in 1968.

Richard A. Rutyna is a native of San Diego, California, but he has lived most of his life in Norfolk, Virginia. He graduated from the Norfolk Division of the College of William and Mary in 1959 with a B.A. in history. He earned his M.A. while a fellow in the history department at the College of William and Mary in Williamsburg. After teaching at Granby High School in Norfolk for one year, he became a member of the history department at Old Dominion, where he still teaches. He is the co-editor of several volumes, including two volumes of essays entitled *Virginia in the American Revolution*, and with John W. Kuehl has also co-edited *Conceived in Conscience: An Analysis of Contemporary Church-State Relations*.

Helicopter Services Courtesy of Atlantic Air Limited; photograph by Robert Firek